Small Business Success

Small Business Success

SMALL
BUSINESS
SUCCESS

Edited by
Paul Foley
and Howard Green

Published on behalf of
the Small Business Research Trust

P·C·P
Paul Chapman
Publishing Ltd

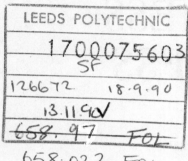
Copyright © 1989 Paul Foley and Howard Green
Chapters 3, 5, 6 and 7 copyright © Paul Chapman Publishing.
Remaining chapters copyright © Paul Foley and Howard Green.

First published 1989
by Paul Chapman Publishing Ltd.
144 Liverpool Road
London
N1 1LA

British Library Cataloguing in Publication Data

Foley, Paul
    Small business success.
    1. Great Britain. Small firms. Management
    I. Title II. Green, Howard, 1922–
    658′.022′0941

ISBN 1–85396–013–6

Typeset by Inforum Ltd, Portsmouth
Printed and bound by St. Edmundsbury Press,
Bury St Edmunds

Contents

Contents   vii

Contributors

Paul Foley
: Lecturer in small businesses and economic development, Department of Town and Regional Planning, University of Sheffield.

Howard Green
: Professor of Planning and Lecturer in small businesses and economic development, Department of Urban Planning, Leeds Polytechnic.

Peter Lovell
: Chief Executive, Barnet Enterprise Trust. Formerly General Manager, London Enterprise Agency.

Colin Mason
: Lecturer in small business and economic geography, Department of Geography, University of Southampton.

Harry Nicholls
: Managing Director and Chief Executive, Birmingham Technology Limited at Aston Science Park.

Alan Pickering
: Chief Executive, Yorkshire Enterprise Ltd.

Acknowledgements

We would like to thank the many individuals, too numerous to name, who have helped us during our research and consultancy on small business growth and development. Their many experiences have provided a rich source of practical advice.

We would also like to thank the Small Business Research Trust for their financial and practical support in the preparation of this book.

Preface

This book is intended primarily for potential and practising small business owners and managers. We have deliberately avoided any precise definition of what constitutes a 'small' business, since any size boundary is inevitably subjective and arbitrary. We anticipate, however, that the tips and strategies contained in the book should assist in the development of any business. The book should also be useful to other groups involved in the development of small businesses, such as business advisers and counsellors and enterprise agencies, and to teachers in educational institutions which run management courses for prospective and established entrepreneurs. In addition, we hope the various professional groups involved in business developments, such as accountants, bankers, solicitors, marketing and management agencies, may find that it helps them to appreciate the problems of developing a successful business from the perspective of the small business owner.

Accelerating interest in business success has led to the publication of a number of books on company development. In general these have examined the development of major corporations or revealed the business experiences of the directors of these corporations. There are remarkably few books which deal with the problems of business development in smaller companies. By drawing together the experience of small business advisers and the experiences of successful small business owners and managers this book seeks to make a unique contribution in filling this significant gap.

1
Introduction

What is sus.

There are over one and a quarter million businesses in the United Kingdom. The vast majority of these are small, employing fewer than 200 employees. Estimates suggest that 93 per cent of all businesses fall into this category. Despite the large number of small businesses and their diverse range of activities they do all have one thing in common: in one way or another they are all striving to become successful. Success in business can be interpreted in many different ways. The most commonly adopted definition of success is financial growth with a high level of profits. However, other definitions of success are equally applicable and many businesses set themselves alternative goals. Some entrepreneurs regard success as the job satisfaction they derive from making a product; this group usually includes skilled craftspeople and artists. Others gain satisfaction and attain success by developing new products; this group may be characterized by inventors and fashion designers. Some groups of workers, such as co-operatives and community businesses, organize themselves with different employment structures to achieve alternative goals.

Many observers and small business writers adopt the traditional view of business success which equates financial growth and a high level of profits with success. The diverse range of criteria which can be adopted to define success can lead many of these observers to view a company as unsuccessful when the owners or managers regard it as highly successful by their own standards. A simple example of this is the large number of companies which remain small because their owners or managers do not want the disbenefits and loss of personal control which sometimes arise with growth. If the owner has an adequate income, job satisfaction, a happy workforce and a stable market position, many would argue that he or she was in a very satisfactory and successful position.

This book is intended to help existing and prospective entrepreneurs and small business advisers to consider the different goals and types of success which small businesses can achieve. The book specifically deals with the strategies, characteristics and activities which small businesses, with their limited financial and manpower resources, can adopt to become successful. The contributors draw on their considerable experience and knowledge as financial, technological and management advisers to many thousands of small businesses. In addition four businesses with different criteria for success are examined to show how they have become successful. The problems and the benefits of the different criteria for success adopted by each business are described.

Chapter 2 examines the different interpretations of success which can be adopted by small businesses. These range from financial success to the more simple pleasures of independence and job satisfaction. In Chapter 3 Colin Mason investigates the distribution of financially successful businesses throughout the United Kingdom. This analysis also examines the distribution of businesses receiving awards for innovation and technological achievements. The study of electrical engineering companies in Chapter 4 shows the diversity of criteria for success which have been adopted and achieved by a representative cross-section of small businesses from the same industry in a single geographical area. Chapters 5–7 are written by contributors who have many years' experience advising large numbers of small businesses. Each contributor has specialized in particular aspects of business development and they use this experience and expertise to provide their views of the activities and strategies which contribute to business success. In Chapter 5 Alan Pickering presents his thoughts on success from a financial viewpoint. Harry Nicholls uses his experience in the development of high technology companies to provide a technological perspective on successful company development in Chapter 6. A more general perspective on the factors contributing to small business success is provided by Peter Lovell in Chapter 7.

Case studies of successful businesses are presented in Chapters 8–11 to highlight the views and experiences of successful entrepreneurs. The case study companies illustrate the range of activities and strategies which have been important in developing successful businesses with different criteria for success. This diversity has been strengthened by selecting companies in varied locations producing different goods and services. Although the case studies have been selected because they illustrate many of the specific issues discussed in earlier chapters, they also reveal the often idiosyncratic approach taken in the development of many businesses.

Kwik-Fit has been included in Chapter 8 because it is one of the United Kingdom's fastest developing financially successful companies. Although no longer small, in the usual sense of the word, Kwik-Fit is still run as a number of individual small depots (businesses) throughout the UK. Tom Farmer, Kwik-Fit's Chairman, has developed the company since its inception and is therefore in a unique position to advise on the development of a financially successful business.

Chapter 9 examines the problems and strategies involved in developing a successful high technology company. Plasma Technology (UK) Ltd was developed by two founders who still manage the company. Its takeover in 1986 highlights one path for continued development which some small businesses adopt.

John Brookfield is the epitome of an entrepreneur who has developed a business which provides him with independence and job satisfaction. Chapter 10 describes his criteria for success and the strategy he has adopted to develop his business.

The final case study, in Chapter 11, describes the development of one of Britain's most successful co-operatives. Its common-ownership philosophy provides an example of company development to achieve an alternative type of business success.

The final chapter draws together all the tips and strategies suggested by the contributors and case study entrepreneurs. It compares the advisers' views with the entrepreneurs' experiences and concludes with five tips for business success.

2
What Is Success?

This book describes strategies, activities and tips involved in developing successful small businesses. Most small business owners and business advisers know there are many different tasks involved in developing a business, each of which has varying degrees of relevance and immediacy. Different strategies and activities need to be adopted at different stages in a company's development to achieve its various goals. It is important for entrepreneurs to know what they want to achieve so they can adopt the appropriate strategy to become successful. Much of the advice given in this book will be valuable in the development of a small business. The advice will be maximized if the various activities are undertaken in a co-ordinated way to achieve specific goals. All the contributors and case study entrepreneurs in the book advocate the use of business plans which clearly specify goals and outline strategies to achieve them. This chapter outlines the different goals and criteria for success an entrepreneur should consider before deciding which will be most appropriate for his or her company. No precise definition of success will be adopted because the balance between factors such as financial rewards, independence, creativity, job satisfaction and happiness is dependent on the attitudes of each individual. It is for the reader to consider the balance between the factors and decide on the goals for his or her business.

Success: a note of caution

Despite the much publicized growth of small businesses in the United Kingdom – there was a net increase of 140,000 between 1980 and 1984 – it is probable that few become successful whatever the criteria for success. The number of business failures – companies which for one reason or another cease trading – is high. Between 1980 and 1984 690,000 businesses ceased trading, representing nearly half the total number of companies in the United Kingdom. Over 30 per cent of companies which start in business cease trading within four years. These figures suggest that the likelihood of survival, let alone success, is low for many companies. However, as this book shows, the chances of survival and success can be enhanced if entrepreneurs have a clear and realistic idea of what they want to achieve and their company adopts appropriate operating procedures.

Financial success

Examples of businesses which were once small but have now achieved considerable financial success are well known. Marks and Spencer, who celebrated their centenary in 1984, started trading from a barrow in Leeds market. The food retailing chain J. Sainsbury was founded in 1869. Examples of successful businesses started in more recent years are also numerous. Barratt Developments, Britain's largest builder of private houses, was formed in 1958. Kwik-Fit, one of the case studies examined in the book, was started in 1971 and now employs almost 2,000 people.

It is becoming increasingly evident that every small business is not striving to become the next multi-million pound small business success. Some entrepreneurs who start with the goal of achieving rapid financial growth re-examine their desire for success when they realize their position in the company can be radically altered as the company grows. Beyond a certain point entrepreneurs have to delegate tasks and relinquish control of parts of their company's operations. At this point the company's success depends on the efforts of other people, not just the entrepreneur's motivation and standards of work. The entrepreneur's role changes into that of a co-ordinator. Continued success depends on the entrepreneur's ability to delegate, recruit the right people and get the best out of them. For some entrepreneurs this challenge is as exhilarating and exciting as the early years of developing the small business. In Chapter 8 of this book Tom Farmer of Kwik-Fit describes how he has adapted to this style of management, and in Chapter 9 David Carr of Plasma Technology (UK) Ltd describes how delegating functions can make the entrepreneur's job more enjoyable. David Carr saw delegation as the opportunity to relieve himself of many of the more mundane tasks of business development to become more involved in the areas he really enjoys.

For some entrepreneurs the loss of direct involvement with day-to-day functions, the increasing difficulties of personnel management and motivating a workforce, and their associated loss in job satisfaction cause them to reconsider the goals for their company. At this point many decide to restrict growth and maintain their company at a size which is manageable for them and from which they obtain a compromise in the rewards of financial income and job satisfaction. One of the company owners interviewed in Chapter 4 clearly recognized the threshold in the development of his electrical engineering business. His company employed 27 people, had a turnover of about £700,000 and provided the founder with a good salary and profits of approximately £50,000 per annum. The entrepreneur clearly decided on his own level of growth stating: 'I own and control a successful company, financially I have few worries and I know all my workforce. Why should I rock the boat? I don't need the money and I certainly don't need the stress and aggravation involved in expanding the company.' Luckily this business was a market where it could consolidate its position without jeopardizing the future of the company. In some industries this is not always possible.

Creativity and independence

Many people are dissatisfied in their current job working for 'someone else'. Some feel restricted because they have no control over the type of work they do, others believe their creativity is being stifled by the organization in which they work. Some decide to do something positive about either or both of these problems and start their own business. Usually this is a carefully considered decision. Sometimes the 'push' to leave work is so great that the decision is taken with little consideration of the longer-term consequences and the business is simply a method of escaping from existing unsatisfactory situations. Even in this case companies can become successful, but the decision to start in business obviously needs to be considered carefully.

The level of independence which can be obtained from starting in business is not always as great as might commonly be thought. An example of the rewards and success which can be achieved is John Brookfield, a case study entrepreneur described in Chapter 10. He felt his innovative talents were being stifled in British Telecom and he was becoming increasingly disenchanted with working in London. So he and his family moved to the Lake District to start their own business. It now has a modest but adequate turnover of £100,000 per annum and the family are very content with their new working environment.

Starting in business may allow entrepreneurs to realize their creative or innovative potential, but at some point products have to be sold and income generated to provide funds to run the business and plan for future development. For fashion designers, computer software designers, potters and other types of craftspeople for whom changing styles and variety in output are a necessity, the creative work in developing products for the business will take a prominent role. Entrepreneurs in these businesses will be able to use their creative talents regularly in the development of the business. For the inventor or innovator the situation is slightly different. Particularly in the high technology area creative input may not be as regular. These people may spend much of their time in the initial phase of the business using their creative skill to develop and refine the product. But once developed they will need to recoup development costs by selling the product. As Harry Nicholls explains in Chapter 6, creative individuals have to realize that at some point they will have to sell their ideas. At this point their job satisfaction and creativity often end and, in their eyes, the hard work begins.

The skills and activities which can best be undertaken to sell new products and develop a 'creative' company are described in later chapters of this book. One feature which constantly emerges is the need to develop marketing skills and spend time selling products. In later years as the company grows it may be possible to delegate this function. There are two main alternatives for those who feel they would not enjoy marketing or sales activities. The first is to start or develop the company in partnership with someone who does enjoy or have experience in this area. The two founders of Plasma Technology (UK) Ltd (see Chapter 9) had complementary skills, one specializing in product design and development and the other in marketing and management. In this way, as the case study shows, each can concentrate in the areas of business in which he has experience and he enjoys. However, it is necessary to emphasize that the relationship between partners is likely to encounter many difficulties as a business develops. If partners decide to leave the business, it will often start to decline. A second alternative, which is really only applicable to inventors of new products, is to sell the rights to produce and sell the product to another company under licence.

Many entrepreneurs start in business to achieve independence and become 'their own boss'. In theory the entrepreneur is entirely independent and free to do whatever he or she desires. The reality of running or developing a small business is slightly different. It is obvious that every company has to sell its products or services. It is through this one activity that, for many entrepreneurs, the independence becomes eroded. To become successful (against a wide variety of criteria) businesses need to satisfy the demands of their customers better than others competing to serve the company's customers. The entrepreneur is therefore free to do whatever he or she wants; but if the company is to become successful it will be dependent on customers. Serving their diverse needs and requirements – when, where, how and at what price they require – is a considerable constraint on the independence of any small business. As one entrepreneur interviewed for this book stated: 'I started this company to become independent; I've never been so beholden to so many people in my life!'

Job satisfaction and other objectives

Implicitly job satisfaction has already been alluded to as a criterion for measuring success. Issues such as independence and creativity are important considerations for many entrepreneurs. Even the disbenefit of a lack of job satisfaction can be discounted by some entrepreneurs if financial rewards are high enough. The views of the individual will influence exactly what he or she regards as job satisfaction. To maximize job satisfaction and achieve other goals some companies have been developed using alternative management and organizational structures. A brief review of these businesses and their objectives shows the wider goals which some businesses are trying to achieve and how they are attempting to maximize job satisfaction.

The best known example of a business with different operating structures and alternative goals is probably the co-operative. The co-operative movement in Britain has a long and chequered history. The first example was started in the eighteenth century when workers from Chatham and Woolwich opened a corn co-operative. Subsequent initiatives involved paternalistic enthusiasts such as Robert Owen who developed the immensely successful Retail and Wholesale Co-operative Societies, which for many epitomized the development of the working-class co-operative movement.

Recent growth in the movement, assisted by the Industrial Common Ownership Fund and the Co-operative Development Agencies, has been rapid. In the early 1970s there were only about 20 co-operatives in Britain. By the mid-1980s there were about 500. Co-operatives usually form in three main ways. Perhaps the most frequent in recent years has been the new business start-up; this is closely followed by the co-operative rescue of a threatened factory or company. Perhaps least significant at present is the third type in which an existing business decides to change the enterprise to co-operative ownership.

Most of the new start-ups, which comprise the majority of co-operatives, are very small, employing fewer than five people. The majority provide services rather than manufacturing a product. Founders usually fall into two main categories: those who feel that the co-operative philosophy fits their own social values and those who want to create their own jobs and see the co-operative approach as a way of doing this.

Equal partners for the common good probably best sums up the philosophy of the co-operative movement. While individual co-operatives have different approaches and constitutions all have the same basic values and guiding principles. Co-operatives are usually structured around six basic principles:

(1) Open voluntary membership.
(2) One-member, one-vote democratic organization.
(3) Limited interest on capital invested within the organization.
(4) Equitable distribution of earned surplus and savings.
(5) Education in co-operative principles.
(6) Co-operation among co-operatives.

Perhaps the major difference between co-operatives and conventional private companies revolves around the issue of the distribution of profit and control. Although some co-operatives employ hired management, ultimate control rests in the constitution of the co-operative: one member, one vote. This is the level at which the organization controls its external environment and this ultimately determines the co-operative's success or failure. In as much as co-operatives operate within a market economy they, like any conventional business, need to control elements of that economy to ensure their success.

Unlike many conventional businesses, for whom profit is a key indicator of performance and success, the co-operative structure can create a Pandora's box of conflicting and competing objectives. The objectives can become all-consuming so that the organization is preoccupied with achieving objectives other than sales or production targets. Leadership is also a key problem for many co-operative organizations. Some choose to ignore the question because it runs counter to the democratic structure of the co-operative ethos. Those which have been financially most successful are often those in which leadership has been clearly defined.

The case study of Suma Wholefoods, in Chapter 11, shows that the generation of profits is not an objective rejected by co-operatives although its significance can often take second place to job satisfaction or other ethically oriented goals.

Another alternative business structure which has developed in recent years has been the community business. These have developed, particularly in Scotland in the past five years, as a response to the problems created by high levels of unemployment. Some local communities suffering from these problems believe that neither the public nor the private sector of the economy will or can do anything to improve their position. As a result they try to help themselves by starting community businesses.

Community businesses are best seen as trading organizations set up, owned and controlled by the local community. They aim to create self-supporting jobs for local people and to be a focus for local development. Any profits made from the business go to create more employment, to provide local services or to assist other schemes of community benefit.

While many writers and pundits applaud the development of community businesses their conflicting objectives can sometimes lead to the dilution of their success. Pricing policy provides one example of the difficulties faced by community businesses. On the one hand community businesses want to ensure a 'fair' return to their community suppliers while on the other hand they are in competition with other businesses for whom concern with the supplier is secondary and price competitiveness is usually paramount.

These types of conflicts are problems which co-operatives and community businesses have to resolve in addition to the normal day-to-day operational difficulties encountered by 'conventional' businesses. Being aware of these problems and recognizing the benefits of this type of company structure are important. The Suma Wholefoods case study, in this book, shows how one co-operative has developed its objectives, adopted sound operating practices and become very successful.

Conclusion

This chapter has identified a variety of objectives and criteria for success commonly adopted by many companies. The use of case studies throughout the book provides examples of how entrepreneurs have developed differing objectives for their companies. Sometimes these objectives have changed as the company has matured, but they have always acted as goals to guide development. Developing objectives and recognizing what the entrepreneur wants from the business are important first steps for any company. It is important for the entrepreneur to know what he or she wants to achieve so that likely problems and opportunities can be anticipated. The activities, strategies and tips contained within this book provide readers with valuable advice about how they can enhance their own chances of success under the criteria for success they have chosen for their company.

3
Where Are the Successful Small Businesses? A Geographical Perspective*

Colin Mason

Introduction

There is clear evidence that different parts of the United Kingdom display contrasts in their capacity for small business formation, survival and success. This chapter is concerned with identifying and explaining these variations between regions and subregions in small business development. It will first describe the geographical differences in new business formation before analysing the traditional dimensions of small business success.

Geographical differences in new business formation

Rates of new business formation (expressed as the number of VAT registrations per thousand employees in each county in the period 1980–3 inclusive) are high throughout most of southern England and also in rural counties of Wales and in the Scottish Islands. The lowest rates are a characteristic of the established urban-industrial areas of northern Britain, notably the North-east, South Yorkshire, West Midlands conurbation, Nottinghamshire, Merseyside, central Scotland and South Wales (Figure 3.1). A broadly similar pattern is in evidence when one considers only the production industries. New firm formation rates are again highest in the South-east region and East Anglia and also in the far South-west, rural West Midlands, mid-Wales and the Scottish Highlands. With

* This chapter is a revised and updated version of a paper which first appeared in *Environment and Planning A* (1985), 17, 1499–1513.

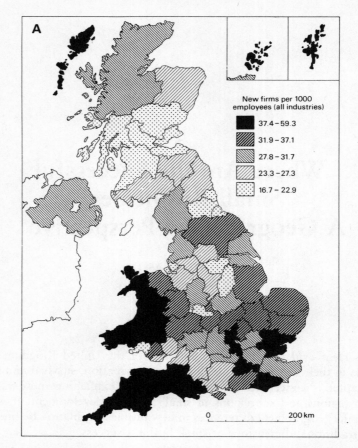

Figure 3.1   New firm formation in all industries in the United Kingdom, 1980–3.

the exception of the Highlands, most of northern Britain is characterized by very low rates (Figure 3.2). Self-employment (as a percentage of total employment) is also highest in southern England. The proportion of the workforce classified as self-employed is above the Great Britain average in the South-east region, East Anglia and the South-west and is lowest in Scotland and the North of England.

Studies of the new firm formation process clearly show that the great majority of new firm founders set up their business in the area in which they are already living and working. The new firm founder who moves to another area specifically to set up a business is extremely uncommon. The reasons for this are twofold. First, knowledge of local markets, potential suppliers, premises and labour market conditions – especially reliable individuals – is greatest in their local area and therefore represents both a key business asset and a method of minimizing uncertainty. Second, many new businesses are started on a part-time basis with the founder maintaining his or her own full-time job. This may also represent a

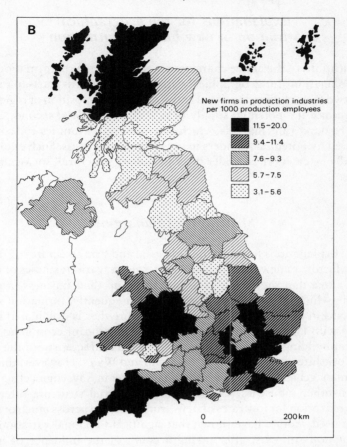

Figure 3.2   New firm formation in production industries in the United Kingdom, 1980–3.

Source: Keeble, D. and Wever, E. (eds) *New Firms and Regional Development in Europe*. Croom Helm, Beckenham, p. 79, Figure 1a.

risk-minimizing strategy, allowing the founder to test the market before committing himself or herself on a full-time basis; alternatively, it might cover the pre-trading stage when the product is being developed. Firms which start on a part-time basis are clearly precluded from any location beyond easy commuting distance from their founder's place of residence. Most part-time start-ups initially operate from the founder's home (spare bedroom, garage, garden hut) and the local ties that are developed in the early stage of the business, notably with customers and suppliers, are likely to restrict any future search for formal business premises to the same locality. Any subsequent relocation of a business (as a result of expansion) is also likely to be highly localized in order to minimize any disruption of trading linkages and to retain employees.

Explanations for the geographical variation in new business formation

The implications of the above characteristics in the new firm formation process is that explanations for geographical variations in business start-up rates must focus on two factors: first, the social and economic composition of regions, since this determines the potential supply of new firm founders; second, the availability of resources and markets, which determine opportunities and constraints encountered by potential founders in the formation process. Such explanations can broadly be categorized under three headings: structural, sociocultural and economic.

Structural explanations

Structural explanations focus on the industrial and firm structures of regions as the major factors in new firm formation rates. First, various studies of new firm founders agree that they tend, as a rule, to set up their business in the same industry in which they previously worked. Consequently, formation rates will be depressed in areas with an industrial structure that is dominated by heavy industries with large capital requirements and significant economies of scale, such as shipbuilding, steel and chemicals. This is a characteristic of the northern region, Yorkshire and Humberside, Scotland and Wales. However, the production and management skills of an individual worker in, say, engineering could be applied in other industries. Consequently, industrial structure offers only a partial explanation for low rates of new firm formation across much of northern Britain. Indeed, studies have shown that significant regional variations in new firm formation still exist after taking account of the influence of industrial structure.

The firm structure of regions (i.e. differences in the proportion of large and small companies), and in particular the proportion of total employment in small and medium-sized firms, is a more significant influence on the rate of new firm formation. Various studies have shown that employees working in small firms and in small subsidiaries of large enterprises have a much higher propensity to start their own firms than do employees in large establishments. One study has estimated that very small manufacturing firms (fewer than 25 employees) spawn new businesses from among their employees at a rate over ten times as high as that from large plants (Fothergill and Gudgin, 1982). The reason would appear to be that employment in a large company does not provide good 'training' for potential entrepreneurs. The hierarchical and occupational employment structures of large companies provide employees wih only a very limited range of work experience. In contrast, employees in small businesses are likely to have direct experience in all areas of their firm's operations. Employees in small firms are also more likely than large firm employees to have contact with customers.

In very small firms the owner is likely to work alongside his or her employees, thereby providing a direct example, or 'role model', for the employees. The greater range of fringe benefits provided by large firms (e.g. company pension scheme, subsidized private health insurance, share option scheme) might also discourage employees from leaving in order to set up their own businesses. The overall effect is to depress rates of new firm formation in areas such as the North of England, parts of the West Midlands, South Wales, Merseyside and central Scotland which have economies dominated by larger companies. Conversely, high rates of new firm formation in areas such as the South-west and East Anglia are at least partly a function of the fact that their industrial structure comprises mainly medium-sized and small firms.

Sociocultural explanations

A sociocultural explanation views regional variations in new firm formation as a product of the 'social climate' and the existing occupational characteristics and socioeconomic mix of the population of a region. These factors are thought to influence the supply of potential new firm founders in a region. There is evidence that an individual's skills and expertise influence his or her ability to establish a viable enterprise. Managerial and professional workers have higher propensities to set up a business than do manual workers on account of their greater commercial, production and managerial skills and enhanced problem-solving abilities. As a result, these groups are more likely to have the necessary self-confidence to initiate and run a successful new business. In addition, their previous work experience is likely to have raised their awareness of sources of outside finance and the ways of presenting a successful case for loan funds. They are also likely to have accumulated adequate collateral against which loans can be secured. Manual workers, on the other hand, are likely to lack the necessary well-rounded commercial expertise and problem-solving skills and find it much harder, or are less willing, to raise external sources of capital.

The high rate of new firm formation in the South-east of England and adjacent counties undoubtedly stems in large measure from its high proportion of managerial, professional and technical occupational groups. This, in turn, is a function of the concentration by large multi-site enterprises of their higher-level managerial and research and development activities in the South-east. Conversely, the rate of new firm formation is depressed in northern England, South Wales and parts of the West Midlands by their high proportions of manual occupations. Furthermore, the numbers of managerial, professional and technical employees in many parts of southern England (e.g. East Anglia and the Solent) have been continually topped up during the past two decades by in-migration from other parts of the country, partly because of the availability of appropriate employment opportunities but also on account of the perceived high residential amenity and environmental quality of such areas. Indeed, the two factors are inseparable as many enterprises have chosen to locate in these areas precisely to enhance their ability to recruit these key groups of workers. The effect of environmentally related population in-migration to parts of southern England has therefore been to enhance its pool of potential entrepreneurs.

The specialized industrial structures of many parts of northern Britain based on mining, steel, shipbuilding and heavy engineering, which persisted into the postwar period, have also contributed to the low rate of new firm formation in such areas. These industries tended to be dominated by a small number of dominant firms in each area, containing a limited white-collar élite. The managerial organization was paternalistic and hence offered few opportunities for individual initiative and advancement. Production techniques often demanded strength, endurance and manual skills rather than independent analysis and judgement. The legacy of this industrial heritage is a proletarian class structure, the absence of an indigenous business class and a reliance on collective, rather than individual, action – in short, a culture that is unfavourable for independent enterprise.

Economic explanations

A third explanation for the geographical variation in new firm formation focuses on the economic advantages and disadvantages of different regions. This perspective argues that new firm formation is influenced by the supply and cost of factors of production (e.g. finance, premises, labour) and by differences in market demand and growth. On both counts the economic conditions in southern England are the most favourable for new firm formation.

First, new firm founders in the South-east have the advantage of superior access to capital. Most new firm founders rely predominantly, or even exclusively, on their own resources. Per capita income levels are higher in the South-east than in all other regions and savings per head of population are also high. Founders often use their house as collateral for raising capital from a bank or other financial institution, or take out a second mortgage. The South-east is again the most favoured region, first on account of its relatively high level of owner-occupation (especially outside Greater London), but more particularly as a result of its high house prices. The opportunities for raising capital in this way are more limited in areas with lower rates of owner-occupation, such as many northern regions, while the amounts of capital which can be raised are limited in regions with low average house prices such as Yorkshire-Humberside, the East Midlands and the North-west. The supply of venture capital is also disproportionately concentrated in the South-east region, which accounted for 47 per cent of recipient companies and 60 per cent of investments by value in 1985. In contrast, Scotland, Wales and the regions of northern England attracted just 17 per cent of venture capital investments.

A further advantage of the South-east region and adjacent counties is the concentration of private and public research establishments. This has contributed to a pool of highly skilled manpower, which provides a much richer network of technical information flows than in other parts of the country and creates greater opportunities for technological transfer from large to small companies and new firm spin-offs by technically qualified employees. The so-called 'Cambridge phenomenon' provides one illustration of this process. Another economic characteristic of southern England that is beneficial to new firm formation is the presence of large numbers of small specialist subcontractors; this enables new firm founders to minimize risk more easily by concentrating on design, assembly, testing and marketing of their product while contracting out the manufacturing processes.

Because most new businesses serve localized markets, a further economic influence on the prospects for new firm formation and growth is the level of demand in the local and regional economy. Once again, the South-east and some adjacent counties have an advantage over other parts of the UK. Measures of regional wealth and household spending power indicate that the size of potential regional consumer demand is highest in the South-east region and lowest in Northern Ireland, Scotland and Wales. Demand from industrial and commercial sectors is also greater in the South of England, in part because of the concentration of relatively prosperous industries such as electronics, defence-related manufacturing and professional and administrative services, and through the centralization of the purchasing functions of larger multi-site enterprises in the South-east of England, which is likely to favour local suppliers. In other regions such demand is often limited because of the contraction of localized industrial complexes in industries such as steel and shipbuilding, and the low level of local purchasing by externally owned branch plants.

The determinants of new enterprise formation are therefore both varied and complex. The industrial and firm size structures of regions are important; so too are the occupational structure and the cultural and social attitudes of the population. Other key factors include the availability of risk capital, the technological infrastructure and the size and growth rates of regional markets. However, the relative importance of each of these factors is unclear, although there is a view that the occupational structure may be the most crucial. Their significance may also vary from region to region. The outcome is marked geographical variations across the United Kingdom in the rates of new business formation, with the highest rates in those counties south of a line from the Wash to the River Avon.

The location of successful small businesses

Many new businesses quickly fail. Analysis of VAT registrations and deregistrations indicates that up to one-third of all new businesses cease trading within three years and nearly half clo _ by their fifth year. Moreover, only a very small proportion of new enterprises which survive for any length of time achieve significant growth. David Storey has claimed on the basis of his research on new manufacturing firms in north-east England that the probability of a new firm having 100 or more employees within 10 years of start-up is between half and three-quarters of 1 per cent (Storey, 1982). This is supported by evidence from the East Midlands that less than 1 per cent of new manufacturing firms started between 1968 and 1975 had over 100 employees by 1975 (Fothergill and Gudgin, 1982). The author's own research in South Hampshire shows that only 1.2 per cent of manufacturing firms started between 1971 and 1979 had over 100 employees by 1985. However, the very small minority of businesses that achieve rapid growth make a disproportionately large contribution to local economic development. These few dynamic new firms accounted for 16 per cent of total employment created by all new start-ups in the period from 1971 to 1979 which survived to 1985. This point is further illustrated by a survey of 52 manufacturing firms in South Hampshire started between 1976 and 1979, which found that three firms accounted for 20 per cent of total employment and 30 per cent of total sales generated by 1981. Moreover, the relative contribution of these rapid-growth firms becomes even more significant over time. A follow-up study of this panel of new enterprises two years later (1983) revealed that the largest three firms accounted for 39 per cent of total employment and 44 per cent of total sales (Mason, 1985).

So, although many new businesses cease trading soon after start-up, and the vast majority of surviving businesses display little or no growth, a very small minority do achieve rapid expansion and make a useful contribution to economic growth and employment creation. However, a comparison of studies of new manufacturing firms in South Hampshire and in the Manchester and Merseyside conurbations suggests that the number of rapid-growth enterprises may vary quite considerably between regions (Lloyd and Mason, 1984). This comparison reveals that the typical new firm in each area is very similar in terms of size (employment, turnover, etc.), market orientation, scale of production, reliance on a small number of key customers, dependence on local market opportunities and lack of innovation. However, there were clear differences between the two areas in the emergence of successful companies. South Hampshire had a handful of rapid-growth new enterprises but these were largely absent from the Manchester and Merseyside group. This finding therefore raises the possibility that rapid-growth new businesses are only found in certain regions and subregions.

Successful small businesses in the United Kingdom

Examination of the location of successful businesses at a national scale is hampered by the lack of comprehensive statistics containing information about the employment and financial performance of small and medium-sized enterprises. However, the use of surrogate measures to identify successful small firms, based first on technical criteria and second on financial criteria, can give some indication of the extent to which such enterprises are concentrated in particular regions and subregions of the United Kingdom. Admittedly, the sources of information used are imperfect. They include recent start-ups and established firms. The criteria of success that are adopted do not invariably equate with rapid growth. Technological innovation does not always result in the rapid employment growth or financial health of the firm. Indeed, a number of studies which have followed through the fortunes of technologically innovative firms have noted that their subsequent performance has often been characterized by difficulty or failure. Equally, a focus on technological innovation overlooks the many fast-growing small firms whose success is based on the application of new concepts of marketing existing products and services. Financial success, in terms of turnover or profit growth, may reflect a recovery situation. Neither need necessarily lead to significant employment creation. Nevertheless, the criteria used below to identify successful small and medium-sized firms do have the merit of being based on a number of objective measures and can therefore be taken as indicative of the location patterns of such firms in the United Kingdom.

The first measure is the number of winners and finalists in various small firm competitions in the early 1980s. The attributes used in judging such competitions relate to technical and design abilities of the firm. They consequently identify a group of enterprises that can be regarded as technological successes. Firms winning such competitions are concentrated in southern England and are largely absent from northern regions (Figure 3.3). The South-east region contains 41 per cent of the total, the South-west has a further 10 per cent and East Anglia has 8 per cent. In contrast, the North, Scotland, Wales and Northern Ireland together contain just 7 per cent of such firms.

However, in order to appreciate the extent to which such firms are disproportionately concentrated in the South of England it is necessary to take account of the underlying distribution of economic activity in the UK. This can be done by calculating 'location quotients' for each region: this simple technique indicates the extent to which a region has more or less than its 'fair share' of a particular distribution, relative to its share of some benchmark activity. In this case the proportion of small firm competition winners in a region is divided by the region's proportion of the national stock of businesses (based on VAT data). If the location quotient is greater than 1 this indicates that the region has more than its 'fair share', a location quotient of less than 1 indicates that it has less than its 'fair share'. The results of the location quotient calculations indicate that East Anglia, the South-west and the South-east all contain more than their 'fair share' of small firm competition winners relative to their shares of the total stock of UK business activity. In the case of East Anglia the location quotient was greater than 3, indicating a substantial overconcentration. All other regions had location quotients of less than 1, with the lowest

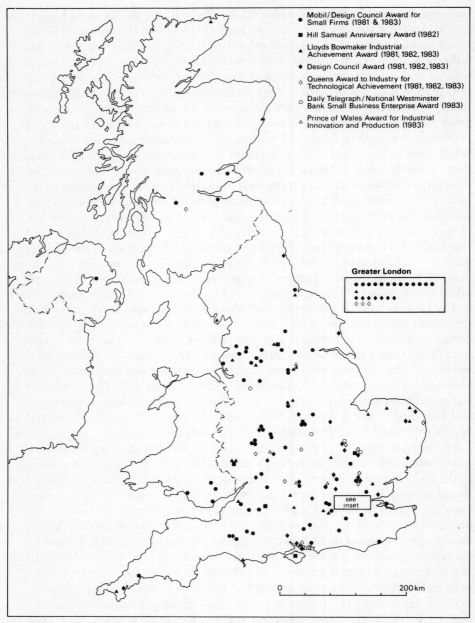

● Mobil/Design Council Award for
  Small Firms (1981 & 1983)

■ Hill Samuel Anniversary Award (1982)

▲ Lloyds Bowmaker Industrial
  Achievement Award (1981, 1982, 1983)

◆ Design Council Award (1981, 1982, 1983)

◇ Queens Award to Industry for
  Technological Achievement (1981, 1982, 1983)

○ Daily Telegraph/National Westminster
  Bank Small Business Enterprise Award (1983)

△ Prince of Wales Award for Industrial
  Innovation and Production (1983)

Greater London

see
inset

0   200 km

Figure 3.3   Small firm competition winners in the United Kingdom, 1981–3.

values in Northern Ireland, Scotland, Wales and the North of England. Hence, the location of small firm competition winners is not simply a reflection of the underlying distribution of economic activity: this group of successful small firms is disproportionately concentrated in southern England.

Successful small and medium-sized firms can alternatively be defined on the basis of financial criteria. One source of information is the *Growth Companies Register 1986* prepared by Growth Data Services Ltd, which lists the 1,000 unquoted companies (including those whose shares are traded on the Unlisted Securites Market and Over the Counter Market) with the highest growth rates in pre-tax profits. The information is drawn from a database of 10,000 companies. Firms must satisfy the following three criteria in order to be included in the register: pre-tax profits in each of the latest three years, minimum pre-tax profits of £50,000 in the latest financial year and consecutive increases in pre-tax profits over the past three accounting periods. Pre-tax profits is a more reliable guide to companies achieving sound expansion than is turnover growth, which may indicate nothing more than overtrading. On the other hand, pre-tax profit figures, especially for small private companies, may be affected by tax planning schemes to boost directors' emoluments while depressing the profits shown in the account. It may also include companies in a recovery phase. Moreover, the fact that only 12 per cent of companies in the 1986 register were also included in the register for the previous year does seem a very high level of volatility. Hence, while this data source does provide a useful guide to financially successful small firms it must also be treated with caution.

Mapping the locations of the 1,000 unquoted companies with the fastest rates of growth in profits by county (Figure 3.4) again highlights their overwhelming concentration in the South-east region. Greater London contained 23 per cent of the total and the rest of the South-east region accounted for a further 21 per cent, with the largest concentrations in Surrey, Essex and Kent. There were also quite significant numbers of such firms in Yorkshire–Humberside (11 per cent) – especially the West Yorkshire conurbation – North-west England (10 per cent), the West Midlands conurbation and Strathclyde. At the other extreme the northern region, Wales and Northern Ireland all contained relatively small numbers. Calculating location quotients confirms that the South-east has a disproportionately large share of fast-growing companies. Yorkshire–Humberside is the only other region with significantly more than its 'fair share' of such firms, made up principally of the large number in West Yorkshire. Most other regions have approximately their 'fair share' of firms. However, Northern Ireland, Wales, the North and South-west of England all have substantially smaller proportions of these financially successful firms than would be expected on the basis of their shares of the total UK business stock.

Another indicator of small and medium-sized companies that can be regarded on financial criteria as successful are those joining the Unlisted Securities Market (USM), which was set up in 1980 to provide smaller, more entrepre-neurial businesses with access to a capital market, but at a lower cost than that

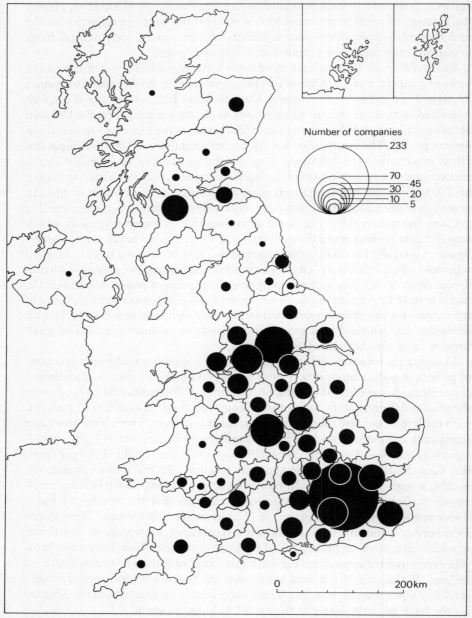

Figure 3.4   Distribution of the 1,000 unquoted companies with the fastest growth in
            profits in the United Kingdom.

Data source: Growth Data Services Ltd (1986) *Growth Companies Register 1986*.

involved in obtaining a full Stock Exchange listing and with less onerous entry requirements. Companies which are admitted to the USM are generally profitable and growing, although 'greenfield ventures' – companies without a trading record but with a fully developed project or product which requires financing – are occasionally accepted.

The geographical distribution of USM companies at April 1985 – excluding subsidiaries, companies registered outside the United Kingdom and companies returning to the Stock Exchange after having had dealings in their shares suspended – is again heavily weighted towards the South-east, which contained 59 per cent of the total, with the next largest share (8 per cent) in the South-west region (Figure 3.5). Companies on the USM in the northern region, Wales, Scotland and Northern Ireland are extremely few and far between. Their combined share is just 7 per cent. The South-east region's share of USM companies in the growth sectors of services (for example leisure, retailing and distribution, public relations and advertising, and television, film and video services) is even greater at 67 per cent, while its share of electronics manufacturing and computer services companies is 72 per cent. The virtual absence of firms in these sectors elsewhere in the UK is equally striking (Figure 3.5). Indeed, it is only with respect to the manufacturing sector, excluding the electronics and instrument engineering categories (where in the South-east the share is only 28 per cent) that there is a significant representation of USM firms in the remainder of the UK. The extent of the overconcentration of USM companies in the South-east of England is confirmed by the fact that it is the only region with a location quotient greater than 1. Every other region has a smaller proportion of USM companies than would be expected on the basis of its proportion of the total UK business stock. Northern Ireland, Wales, the North of England and Scotland are again the regions which are most underrepresented in terms of their relative shares of USM companies.

Conclusion

There are marked variations in small firm start-ups across the UK, which appear to stem from differences between regions in industrial and firm size structures, sociocultural attributes, availability of resources and market opportunities. This chapter has sought to demonstrate that there are even greater variations between areas in terms of their numbers of successful small firms. These firms are disproportionately concentrated in the South-east region and underrepresented in most peripheral regions of the UK, notably Northern Ireland, Scotland, Wales and the northern region of England. A location in any of these regions does not prevent a firm from achieving success. Indeed, Figures 3.3–3.5 indicate that there are successful firms in the peripheral regions of the UK. However, in terms of weight of numbers such firms are overwhelmingly found in the South-east region where the share of successful small firms is much greater

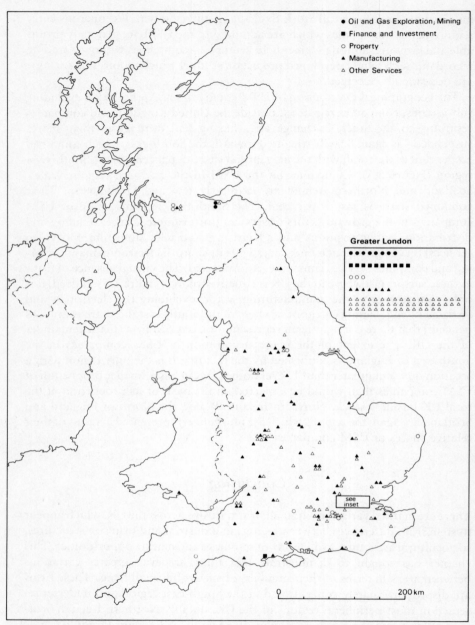

Figure 3.5   Distribution of companies on the Unlisted Securities Market, April 1985.

than 'expected' on the basis of its proportion of the UK business stock.

Reasons for this location pattern are open to speculation but seem likely to reflect several factors. One possibility might be the difficulties encountered by firms in peripheral regions in obtaining venture capital, although there are many examples of successful small firms financed largely through internal sources, topped up by a bank loan and overdraft facilities. A more significant consideration may be the limited local market opportunities in northern regions. The high levels of consumer wealth in the South-east region and its leading role in initiating new fashion trends provide much greater market opportunities for small firms, especially innovative ones, than are available elsewhere in the UK. The concentration of government laboratories, industrial research organizations and research and development establishments of large, private-sector organizations in the South-east provides a source of innovative demand pull for small businesses that is largely absent from other regions.

These factors can, and are, being tackled by policy-makers, albeit with varying degrees of success. For example, technical enterprise boards and local venture capital funds have increased the supply of risk capital. 'Meet the buyer' and 'Can you make it?' exhibitions are seeking to increase market opportunities for small businesses. Science parks and innovation centres have been established to foster the transfer of technology from educational establishments to small and medium-sized firms. However, arguably the most important reason for the existence of geographical variations in the location of successful small firms reflects the occupational structure of regions, which is a much more difficult issue for policy-makers to solve. A number of studies have suggested that as a general rule the fastest growing small firms are run by owner-managers who have managerial backgrounds, frequently in marketing or technical areas. As already noted, the South-east region (and some adjacent counties) has the highest proportion of managerial, professional and technical occupational groups, mainly because large corporate enterprises tend to locate their high level managerial functions in this region. Consequently, in the South-east the pool of potential founders with the necessary industrial and commercial experience and knowledge to start businesses which have the potential to achieve rapid growth, is much greater than in all other parts of the UK.

The most appropriate method of increasing the numbers of individuals with the potential to start firms which will achieve rapid growth is likely to be through enterprise training (in the broadest sense of the term). The record on enterprise training is that it can promote 'entrepreneurship' among individuals, smooth the transition from employment into self-employment and reduce failure rates. However, the extent to which it can convert a potential new firm founder, or even a low-performing small business owner-manager, into a 'high flier' is debatable, not least because the precise attributes of small business success are currently poorly understood. Some of these attributes are discussed in the remaining chapters of this book.

References

Fothergill, S. and Gudgin, G. (1982) *Unequal Growth: Urban and Regional Change in the UK*, Heinemann, London.

Lloyd, P.E. and Mason, C.M. (1984) Spatial variations in new firm formation in the United Kingdom: comparative evidence from Merseyside, Greater Manchester and South Hampshire, *Regional Studies*, Vol. 18, pp. 207–20.

Mason, C.M. (1985) The development of new manufacturing firms, *International Small Business Journal*, Vol. 3, no. 2, pp. 33–45.

Storey, D.J. (1982) *Entrepreneurship and the New Firm*, Croom Helm, Beckenham.

4
Small Business Success –
a Market Survey

Paul Foley

Preceding chapters have shown a wide variety of goals and criteria which can be used to measure small business success. Very little is known about the relative importance of the different criteria for success which new and established small businesses are trying to achieve. Traditionally economists, policy-makers and others assume that all small businesses want to become multi-million pound successes. This assumption has been questioned in recent years by the realization that not all businesses desire this level of growth and even fewer businesses have the ability to achieve it. Many are happy to remain trading at a level which provides acceptable levels of financial reward or job satisfaction for the owner-manager and/or employees.

A review of small businesses from one industry in one geographical area enables the diversity of goals among a cross-section of companies to be analysed. The analysis was undertaken as part of a project to investigate the attributes contributing to small business success. In this chapter the characteristics and goals of the small businesses are described first, before discussing the attributes which financially successful and growing companies possessed.

The companies interviewed

Interviews were conducted with 61 out of a total of 91 small electrical engineering businesses (fewer than 200 employees) in North and West York-shire to discuss their trading patterns and attitudes towards success. The average size of the companies interviewed was 25 full-time employees. The contrast in the desire for success and growth is best shown by the attitudes of the smallest and the largest company.

The smallest company, located in Huddersfield, started in 1920 and at its peak employed eight people. When interviewed the last remaining employee was the 75-year-old manager who was the son of the founder of the company. He had been with the company for almost 50 years. The eight employees which the company possessed under his management in 1950 was the maximum he could tolerate. He believed that with more than eight employees the problems of personnel management and the associated delegation of activities were unnecessary burdens which could be avoided. To maintain his own job satisfaction and the camaraderie among his friends in the workforce he decided to restrict the size of the company. Since 1950 employees had left or retired from the company at regular intervals. He had considered retiring but realized the company was really his only interest. He decided that while he still enjoyed working he would continue with the company. Although he now admitted to running the company more as a hobby than a business it continued to operate on a commercial basis and records a small profit each year. His only concession to his age has been to develop carefully the market for his products in Wales. He has a small holiday cottage in North Wales and always tries to spend a week in the cottage after making deliveries to his Welsh customers.

The largest company, located in the North Yorkshire town of Knaresborough, was developed from the spark of an idea which the founder had while driving home one evening in 1962. Having almost collided with some roadworks, due to the failure of the paraffin lights which were supposed to be illuminating the scene, he realized that there was a more efficient way of lighting roadworks and subsequently went on to develop flashing beacons which are now used throughout the UK construction industry. Having 'succeeded' and made a considerable personal fortune he did not sit back and rely on one product. He quickly became aware that although having been the first into the market it was quickly becoming saturated with other suppliers. The company has subsequently diversified into a variety of other electronic products. The founder's 'business acumen' and ability to spot growth markets enabled the company to become one of the first in the UK to produce printed circuit boards. When interviewed in 1983 it had a turnover of more than £3m per annum and employed 198 people. It had doubled its size in the preceding five years. The company has continued to expand under the guidance of the founder and it now employs 300 people. The company plans to maintain its current expansion rate and provides a fine example of the growth and success which many people believe all small businesses are striving for.

Interviews with the 61 companies showed that the two companies described above represent the two extremes of businesses with a wide diversity of goals. This diversity is apparent even when companies first start trading. When asked why they started in business 60 per cent described a desire for independence or the need to find an outlet for their own abilities as a major consideration. Eighteen per cent saw the development of a market opening as a reason for starting. Even fewer, 8 per cent, had financial ambition as a motivating factor.

The overriding reason for starting in business seems to concern intrinsic satisfactions, the most important of which are personal autonomy at work and independence. The extent to which independence exceeds the more traditional view of all small businesses aspiring to become financially successful is perhaps surprising. However, there seems to be a clear understanding among many small business owner-managers that there is a threshold level at which they can optimize their own job satisfaction without exceeding their management capabilities.

The circumstances affecting individual companies, their achievements and goals do not remain static. The owner-manager's view about his/her company changes as the company develops. Changing circumstances, the development of sales and increased financial rewards might have been expected to change the owner-manager's values and perception of the benefits of managing a small business. This was certainly not the case among the companies interviewed. The importance of independence and the ability to find an outlet for their own abilities were seen as the main benefits of managing a small business by 87 per cent of owner-managers, 27 per cent more than when the companies first started in business. Although this does not preclude the additional benefits of financial rewards derived for the owner-manager, only 5 per cent of interviewees explicitly mentioned this as important.

The traditional view that all small businesses want to grow and become multi-million pound successes appears to be a mistaken one. Very few companies have the desire, let alone the ability, to achieve this level of success. Owners and directors in the companies interviewed were asked what would be the ideal size for their company with them remaining in their present management position. Only six (12 per cent of all companies) felt they had the desire to operate in any size of company, but even one of these added that he would divide the company into units of 120 employees. A further seven said they would be happy with 100–200 employees. The remaining companies, which comprised three-quarters of all those interviewed, had a more limited desire for growth. The ideal average company size among this latter group was only 27 employees. Many owners and directors voiced the opinion that approximately 27 employees was an optimum size beyond which they would have to delegate managerial responsibility for major areas of the company's operations. By restricting the size of the company they could retain control of nearly all the company's activities. This was probably the most important reason for restricting the growth of many companies. Several interviewees were also quick to point out that even a relatively small company with 27 employees in the electrical engineering industry should achieve sales of approximately £700,000. At this level they could receive a good salary and the company could make profits of approximately £50,000. By restricting the size of the company they could retain the business at a 'manageable' size and receive satisfactory financial rewards. As one owner clearly stated: 'I own and control a successful company. Financially I have few worries and I know all my workforce. Why should I rock the boat? I don't need the money and I certainly don't need the stress and aggravation which would be involved in trying to expand the company.'

The companies' analysis of success

The 61 electrical engineering companies were asked which attributes they thought characterized successful companies. The analysis primarily investigated success from a financial viewpoint. However, it was interesting to note that even among companies striving to achieve alternative goals, such as job satisfaction or independence, there was agreement that they should plan for the future and have a clear idea of their objectives or goals. The need for adequate business planning was the main attribute which contributed to success. Many believed that only by clarifying what the owner or director wanted to achieve could the company plan for the future and develop a strategy or trading pattern to achieve the desired level of success. This view was shared by growing companies as well as by those wanting to consolidate their position and maintain or reduce their present size. By identifying clear goals companies could identify which elements of their strategy or trading pattern were advantageous and which were detrimental to their success. Seventy-one per cent of companies believed it was necessary and beneficial to plan for the future. However, nearly half (46 per cent) had no plans or goals for the future. Some of these companies were trading effectively and making a profit. Most had been operating in the same way for many years. Many owners were often happy that things had not changed. However, during interviews it became clear that in recent years some owners and directors had not considered what they wanted to achieve with the business. For many the interview provided them with their first opportunity to 'sit back' and consider the wider issues concerning the future of the company rather than dealing with the day-to-day issues involved in running the business. Many found the opportunity to consider the wider issues of running the company to be a useful exercise. Several commented that they would develop their ideas and try to 'break' their routine of running the business in a relatively aimless way.

Plans for the future were thought to be useful by more than 70 per cent of companies interviewed. Business planning was thought to be particularly valuable by companies which had achieved a high level of financial success. Even among companies striving for success in ways other than financial, such as maintaining an optimum size, planning for the future and the adoption of goals and objectives were thought to be beneficial exercises. Whatever a company's criteria for success, business plans and performance targets provide a benchmark against which to evaluate performance. Company strategy and operating patterns can be evaluated against plans to assess whether elements are beneficial or detrimental to success. Companies operating on a day-to-day basis respond to problems as they arise. This approach makes them prone to unfavourable

trading patterns. Business plans and the regular appraisal of company performance against desired targets can avoid this problem.

The review of a business plan, which should be undertaken on a six-monthly
to yearly basis, assesses how a company has performed against a set of
previously developed business plan targets. Strengths and weaknesses in the
company's operations can be identified. Areas where the company has failed to
achieve targets can be examined and new measures can be taken to overcome the
weaknesses. Equally, the company's strengths can be acknowledged. The review
process can also be used to identify new opportunities. Action can also be
planned to minimize the effect of any threats to the company's trading position.
Putting ideas on paper helps to concentrate the mind; it also ensures that there is
clear documentary evidence of previous ideas at each review. The business plan
does not have to be a very long document, although if time permits extra detail
can help to outline the company's plans more clearly. At the very least a business
plan should contain details of the company's goals and objectives, a broad
outline of how these will be achieved together with budgets for the future.

Analysis of the factors contributing to success

The main purpose of interviewing the electrical engineering companies was to
investigate the factors which contribute to their financial success. Seven different
measures of financial success were adopted. These ranged from the common
indices of sales and profit used in most financial analysis, to other measures,
such as turnover on assets and profit per employee, which took account of the
different sizes of companies interviewed. Statistical analysis identified those
factors which made the greatest contribution to financial success. These results
were verified by comparing the attributes of the most successful companies
against those of the other companies interviewed.

Analysis consistently showed that three main attributes were important in
contributing to small business success. The first was the development of new
products. Many companies found it more profitable to develop and exploit new
markets with new products than they did to enter markets where there was
already competition.

The second important attribute was the number of sales and marketing staff
employed by the company. The number of personnel in these activities usually
showed a clear commitment to effective marketing. This was important because,
as one businessman stated, 'even the best products do not sell themselves'. The
benefits of the third attribute, business planning, were outlined in the previous
section. A review of the best and worst performing companies shows why these
attributes are important.

The exploitation of a new product or idea was a common feature among the
most successful companies. These companies were also usually very keen to

diversify from being reliant on a single product. One founder who lived in London recognized that the growth of plant hire shops in the South of England in the early 1960s had not taken place in the North. He saw a gap in the Yorkshire market and opened several shops. Shortages in the supply of generators led him to start manufacturing these as a method of diversifying the company's operations. The company has subsequently gone on to manufacture a variety of other electrical goods. As the founder pointed out: 'The plant hire market has now become saturated by the "big boys" who were originally confined to the South. I knew I had to take advantage of that opportunity and realized it would not last for ever, so I exploited other markets and opportunities as I saw them.'

The ability of the most successful companies to recognize the limitations of their first market and take advantage of other opportunities or market niches was very common. The exploitation of ideas or new markets, as one company founder pointed out, was not always an easy task. This managing director, whom one of his colleagues described as 'a fountain of ideas', stressed that although he had developed a wide range of new products, the key to the company's success was effective marketing. He knew his skills lay in developing products but he believed his ideas would come to nothing unless they were properly marketed and exploited. Therefore, over a period of several years, he appointed a very experienced marketing team who provided the company with a well-planned marketing management strategy. The managing director stated that 'although they (the marketing team) often sit on my ideas, taking ages to develop marketing plans and produce them, that's exactly what I appointed them for. Without their moderating influence we would not be half as successful as we are today.' The company is now a market leader in intercom systems, alarms and communication equipment for hotels and homes for the elderly.

The compromise between developing new ideas and products, which many managers seem to enjoy, and the 'hard' but essential task of marketing is perhaps best illustrated by one company started by a university lecturer in 1974. The company was developed from the chemistry lecturer's hobby as a radio 'ham'. Having advertised various items of radio equipment, which he made at his home, in radio magazines he decided to leave his job and exploit the ideas commercially. He says he finds marketing management 'a very necessary chore. Good new products almost sell themselves, but to be successful the company needs a well planned market strategy.' He therefore tries to split his time equally between his 'hobby' of developing new products and the 'business' of marketing. In the future he hopes to take on marketing staff, but when interviewed he believed the company could not afford them. In many ways this company epitomized the characteristics and attributes of the successful companies. In spite of its relatively small size (only 14 employees) it was performing the same functions and had characteristics very similar to those of its larger even more successful counterparts.

Among the ten most successful companies (in terms of both financial and employment growth) one company stood out as an exception when looking at the general characteristics of all the others interviewed. This electric blanket manufacturer did not have a new product. It had no explicit form of business planning. Only 2 of its staff of 30 were concerned with marketing. The managing director was 73 years old. This company appeared to have few, if any, of the characteristics required for success. The managing director, who had been with the company for over 30 years, was undoubtedly the driving force behind the company. It was his influence which had enabled the company to achieve and maintain its turnover of £600,000 per annum and profit level of £80,000 per annum. His knowledge of the market and of his competitors was astounding. Although under formal criteria the company possessed no form of business planning, the managing director's knowledge and single-minded desire for success meant that the company appeared to be one of the best managed firms visited. The managing director had a clear idea of what the company required and he implemented his ideas rigorously. He regarded marketing as very important for his company in its early development. The company had established itself among only four other major UK suppliers of electric blankets. He believed little could be done to improve its position without a major national advertising campaign, which he estimated would cost over £500,000. Even then he was doubtful that his customers, who comprised major high-street retailers such as British Home Stores, Currys and Boots, would increase their orders. This, he believed, was because the majority of customers preferred to purchase electric blankets from a mixture of the five major suppliers to ensure competition and supply. They were thought to be reluctant to rely on just one major supplier.

The managing director's main reason for staying with the company well beyond the usual retirement age was because he wanted to see the company diversify its activities and also because he wanted his daughter, who had recently joined the company, to take over a thriving company. The company was therefore considering the development of new products. The managing director stated that when the company diversified, a sound marketing management strategy would be an essential requirement to establish the product.

Although initially the company did not appear to have the main attributes of the other successful companies, closer examination of its past, present and possible future development revealed that the managing director, marketing management policies and desire for growth were not dissimilar from those of the other successful companies interviewed. This 'exception' does, therefore, appear to conform to many of the characteristics identified in the other successful companies.

The successful companies had a dynamism, with a feeling of success, and clear desire for further growth. They were well managed, with clear plans for the future and good marketing management policies. None of these attributes was readily apparent in the least successful companies. Many were on the verge of failure and seemed to be unaware of some of the very basic mistakes they were making. Many of the least successful companies were managed by individuals who appeared to lack drive or ambition. Most were aware they were performing badly, but did not know how to overcome their problems.

One company which employed 44 people in 1977 had only 12 when visited. The company manufactured dynamos and alternators and blamed its decline 'on the general reduction in the economy'. The owner adopted a very product-orientated approach, believing that if a good product was being produced at a reasonable price they should have few problems. He believed marketing was unimportant and said that 'planning is important for some companies, but because we cannot control our market it is unnecessary'. He also went on to say that they were 'struggling to survive', 'reducing prices to get business' and 'spent as little as possible on marketing'. This company was one of the least successful visited. The owner of the company was 57 years old and seemed to lack both the desire and marketing knowledge to prevent the company's decline.

The age of the manager was undoubtedly one reason for the acceptance of decline in some of the least successful companies. One company which manufactured transformers had been making a loss for two years. The managing director said that his goal was to recoup these losses and keep going for another five years and then retire. He complained of competition from overseas and said he had thought about diversifying but had 'never done anything about it'. He stated that 'we should really plan for the future. But what's the point at my age? I retire soon.' The company had made one of the major mistakes which affected many of the least successful businesses. They were very reliant on one customer for business, in this case British Rail. When British Rail found other suppliers the company was badly affected and had to make several staff redundant. The company does not seem to have learnt from its mistake; it now sells 60 per cent of its only product to GEC.

Another managing director who was 55 years old said that he became 'less motivated about running the company as time goes on'. He stated that he would like to sell the business, but because no one would buy it he was 'stuck with it'. He believed that the company would not grow 'unless someone with a lot of ambition joins us'. Since they 'could not afford to take on new staff' this was highly unlikely. The need for planning and marketing in larger companies was acknowledged by the managing director. However, he did not think it was appropriate for a company with only 16 employees. He even went on to say that 'highly marketing orientated firms can do very well, but we only work on a day to day basis with no planning'. Probably the most startling comment he made was that they were 'not looking for any more business, because (their) old customers would come back' to them. The company had been recording a loss for the past three years.

The picture painted by the least successful companies was generally very gloomy, but like the 'successes' earlier, one firm did stand out as an exception. The company manufactured hi-fi speakers and was among the ten least successful companies (in terms of both financial and employment growth). The company started in 1973 and reached a peak employment of 47 in 1976. When visited it employed only 22 people. The company had been making a 'large loss' and was facing considerable cash flow problems. The managing director had sold a large proportion of the equity in the business to overcome these problems. The two new partners, who had taken the equity stake in the company, revised the managerial structure and operations of the company. The managing director stated that the company 'had been in the market a long time, but until the arrival of the new people marketing was not as good as it should have been. They (the new partners) gave the company a major marketing boost.' For the first time the company now had a written business plan and plans to diversify into new markets in order to overcome seasonality in the hi-fi market. The company was on course to making a profit again and was now having problems meeting increasing product demand.

Conclusion

Many of the most successful companies are concerned with the exploitation of new products. However, the majority are also aware of the need to market their products effectively and take maximum advantage of their market position. Planning is usually very important to these companies and many have pursued long-term goals to diversify and develop new markets before their existing markets become saturated. As the communications company set up by the university lecturer showed, the size of a company does not appear to restrict the development of good marketing practices. The most important attributes of all the successful companies were not only their ability to perform all of the above functions well, but also their desire for growth and success.

A desire for growth was often missing from the least successful companies. Many provide worryingly good examples of bad management practice. Very few managers saw a need for marketing policies in 'their' business and few possessed any experience in this area. However as the last case study, the hi-fi loudspeaker manufacturers, showed, it does appear to be possible to reverse the fortunes of even the worst performing company if good management practices are adopted.

Five tips for success

(1) Decide how you want the company to develop and what rewards you want to obtain from the business (financial, social and others).
(2) Prepare and review business plans on a regular basis. Use the reappraisal process as an opportunity to review goals and objectives and to identify strengths and weaknesses in the company.
(3) Know the market and identify what it is the customers want to buy. Use this

information to develop marketing management policies to maintain or exploit the company's position within the market.

(4) Be aware of opportunities to develop new products which fill a gap in the market.

(5) Do not rely heavily on one customer and consider carefully all the consequences of accepting the 'big order'.

5
Successful Businesses – The Financial View

Alan Pickering
Chief Executive, Yorkshire Enterprises Ltd

Alan Pickering graduated in economics at Cambridge and has since then divided his activities between merchant banking and business. He joined the West Yorkshire Enterprise Board at its inception in 1982 and, as managing director, was instrumental in establishing its present structure.

Following the abolition of the metropolitan counties in 1985 he has steered the Board to its now well-respected role as a venture capital house of major significance under its current trading name of Yorkshire Enterprises Ltd.

Introduction

In the world of small business, the mortality rate of new firms can be as high as 33 per cent within two years of starting or 60 per cent within five years. Against this background the first question that will be considered by any individual or institution asked to finance a new business will be: 'What are its prospects for survival in the medium to long term?' Before setting up a business, aspiring entrepreneurs should already have asked themselves that question in as many different forms as they can devise.

Developing the business – the business plan

The first steps in developing a successful business are to research the project thoroughly and to seek informed and professional advice on as many aspects as possible. The results of this process must be distilled into a comprehensive and coherent business plan. The plan need not be compiled in great detail over a long timescale. For example, cash flow projections are unlikely to turn out to be even remotely accurate beyond two years. However, the principal objectives and limitations should be assessed for up to five years ahead.

The discipline of conducting this exercise thoroughly will produce two vital results. First, it will tell entrepreneurs whether their initial optimism was well founded or whether there are likely to be any basic problems which they did not know or consider in the first flush of enthusiasm. Second, the business plan will set the strategic objectives of the enterprise for a number of years ahead and provide a background framework against which future decisions can be taken when initial plans have to be modified or discarded in the hard reality of the market-place.

The first and last problem in business development: finance

In one sense, the finance needed for a project is the first problem to be tackled. Without finance nothing can happen and without an assured availability of the full finance needed, nothing should happen. Very few people are fortunate enough to have the resources to both start and develop their own business without involving finance from third parties. Most find themselves in the position of having to convince financiers, banks, sources of venture capital or providers of grants that their support is deserved. They will certainly not succeed in doing so unless their proposals are well thought out, tested so far as is reasonably possible, well presented in an easily absorbed summary and then 'sold' by a person who shows commitment and enthusiasm tempered by realism and sound judgement.

So the first problem becomes the last. The advisers will help to test the proposals, to cost out their financial implications and to produce the presentation. Only then should the entrepreneur approach external sources of finance.

Sources of finance

One of the principal reasons for the creation of Enterprise Boards and similar organizations was the existence of a 'funding gap' for small businesses. It was first identified in a study in the 1930s but little was done until the 1950s. The clearing banks then funded an organization, the Industrial and Commercial Finance Corporation, intended to provide long-term, fixed-asset investment capital. This was to complement the clearing banks' own overdraft finance which had always been, at least in theory, short term and intended to finance only working capital such as stock and debtors. While this move vastly improved the supply of long-term loans it still left a gap in the provision of 'risk capital', particularly in smaller amounts.

Over the past seven years that provision has improved rapidly. Subsidiaries of banks are now willing to invest longer-term finance that is not always fully secured. The Loan Guarantee Scheme was introduced to provide further help. However, the fact that this scheme involves the banks in taking an equity type of risk without an equity return has tended to limit its effective deployment. Still more recently have been the creation of local or regional financial organizations, some public sector, some private, and an increasing interest from local authorities seeking to support employment in their areas.

While provision continues to improve in these ways, the equity funding gap for new or young small firms continues to persist – principally because the private sector must pay attention to alternative rates of return which will always be higher and faster in larger, fast-growth businesses. Equally, while public-sector organizations or local enterprise trusts will be less demanding in the returns that they seek and more willing to provide long-term finance in small amounts, they are also constrained by the heavy personnel costs involved in the appraisal and monitoring of investments. The government is currently introducing a pilot scheme to provide support personnel from its Small Firms Service to some Local Enterprise Agencies with the intention of assisting and encouraging providers of small-scale risk capital to increase the range of their activities.

Nevertheless, there is a great demand for the highly skilled and experienced personnel needed for the appraisal and monitoring of investments and a relatively low availability. These pressures will mean that the administrative cost of providing small-scale risk capital is likely to remain very high in both relative and absolute terms. As a result, the City of London finance sources find themselves unable to consider small investments and the anomaly has arisen that institutions specializing in the provision of small-scale equity investment are as much in need of a subsidy or grant as the recipients!

In summary, the provision of small-scale risk capital is likely to remain patchy and variable across the country. Demand is growing steadily because of the increasing rate of new business formation and it will probably continue to outrun supply, even for proposals which may be very attractive in everything but their small scale. In these circumstances, entrepreneurs must take increasing care in both the preparation and presentation of their case for support.

What makes a successful business?

The answer to this question will be quite different according to whether it is given by a proprietor/director, a customer, a creditor, an economist or a provider of finance.

However, the author is concerned with the answer as seen by the provider of finance. Broadly speaking, the higher and faster the anticipated financial return the more attractive the business will be to the provider of equity finance. The provider of loan capital, by contrast, will be more concerned with the security cover for its lending in the event of failure. The better the security the lower will be the interest charge and the greater the willingness to lend for the medium or long term.

Public-sector agencies may often be the most attractive source of small-scale risk capital. Their primary objective of the 'social return' from increased employment opportunities means that they are usually more willing to accept a lower level and speed of return on their risk investments. Although the public sector places a different emphasis on its own investment objectives from the private sector, this does not mean that it looks for different attributes of success in the business in which it invests. Basic objectives will be held in common by both sectors: first, survival in the early years; second, steady and sustainable growth in profitable activity over the medium and long term. The private sector will be more interested in the implications for its own rate of return on investment. The public sector will be more interested in the consequent growth of employment. Both will be looking for sustained growth and both are likely to have similar views on the means by which that objective is most likely to be attained.

Attributes of success

There is a saying among venture capitalists that five things matter in a business. The first three are management, management and management. The fourth is market and the fifth product. As with most aphorisms it oversimplifies. Many other points could be added to the specification. Two which must be added are controls and finance. These are reviewed separately in the remainder of this chapter.

Management

The fundamental importance of good management cannot be exaggerated. Poor, untrained or inexperienced management can ruin the best business. Conversely determination, skill, experience and good judgement can make a success of many an unlikely prospect.

Investors look for leadership, balance, depth and coherence in a management team. Some of these requirements are extremely difficult for the small business to meet because it cannot support the overhead implied. Often the proprietor may be the sole senior manager in a small business. In the early days there is nobody to whom they can delegate. The danger is that they will find themselves psychologically unable or unwilling to delegate as their business grows. They must resist the temptation to continue to run a growing business as a one-person band. They must do their best to recruit or train people who can provide the specialist support that growth entails in marketing, sales, production, finance and all the other specialist skills. If the business cannot afford to recruit them it will be essential to develop the strengths and confidence of junior employees so that they can accept increasing levels of responsibility.

The problems of development and delegation in management must be handled correctly. If they are not and the business remains small, it will be exposed to the dangers attendant on static growth. If the business grows without expanded and balanced management there will be the even greater danger of a loss of control and cohesion leading only too easily to unexpected, sudden and unnecessary disaster. The evidence is overwhelming that many senior management failures occur in the transformation from a large/small business to a small/large one. It is not easy to judge when the change of scale is occurring and too often it goes unattended until serious management problems surface. This may be because the type of person suited to running a small business is quite inappropriate to the running of a large one, and no entrepreneur will be easily convinced that the business he or she has built up should be run by somebody else. Nevertheless, if the entrepreneur cannot adapt, then he or she should be replaced because he or she is unlikely to be able to recruit and retain high-quality managers if they are not given the appropriate responsibility and authority.

Market

The most common business mistake of all is that to which the inventor is prone: creating a new product and only then researching the market. To say this is not intended to dampen the enthusiasm of inventors, only to warn that the problems of manufacturing and marketing a new product successfully may be much greater than those involved in designing and producing the prototype in the first place. However, there are many ways to overcome them, such as licensing and corporate venturing.

The relevance of marketing to most businesses is basic. Sales are the life-blood of any business and securing them depends on discovering, researching and addressing potential markets correctly. The market for a new product may be too small to be exploited commercially. The market for an existing product may go into permanent decline. Then the business must be capable of adjusting by finding new markets or replacement products for the existing market, otherwise cutback, decline and eventual disaster will be inevitable.

The tragedy for much of British industry in the recession of 1979–81 was the large number of production-oriented businesses left floundering by a large rise in sterling exchange rates. In some cases this reduced export potential, in others it increased the invasion of home markets by growing international competition. Businesses which had enjoyed apparently secure markets for many years were left helpless. This was particularly true of the many engineering firms whose function was mainly that of subcontract suppliers making parts for the end-products of others. When these orders dwindled they had no research and development capacity to turn to, no marketing organization to defend them and no future other than cutback or closure.

Perhaps the prime example was the motor vehicle industry. There was a slow, long-term decline of British Leyland's market share in the face of Japanese imports throughout the late 1970s. When the market suddenly went into recession, this became the main cause of a wave of closures of small and medium-sized firms in the West Midlands. Since then, of course, the wheel has come full circle with an improvement in exchange rates increasing the prospects of British exports abroad.

Products

A company's products may consist of anything from an individual personal service to the manufacture of large capital equipment. Although, in terms of attaining success, entirely different productive factors will be needed across the range, the principles underlying provision of the output will not. The product must be made available in the appropriate quantity saleable, to the correct specification and quality and then delivered when required by the customer. Costs must allow both adequate profit and a selling price acceptable in the market-place. The technical and other inputs required must all be available otherwise any marketing efforts will be wasted. Any investor must judge the likelihood of the business achieving these objectives within its existing and anticipated human, material and financial resources.

Controls

A key requirement of successful management is the ability to devise, design, implement and operate the various controls needed to achieve the objectives of the business.

The operational controls required will vary widely, both in range and relative importance, from one business to another and can only be described in detail in the context of the particular business under consideration. However, some controls are basic and should be common to all businesses whatever their criteria for success. The primary controls are the operating and financial ones appropriate to the trade. They should be as simple, direct and immediate as possible. Their purpose and method of implementation must be clearly under-stood by all those concerned in both operating them and in responding to their discipline. Equally they must be used and seen to be used effectively.

Most important of all, the necessary financial control information must be made available promptly at the correct intervals and monitored regularly and thoroughly by all the managers concerned. Nothing is more futile than a large administrative bureaucracy that produces a mass of undigested information that managers or directors do not have the time or inclination to read. Conversely a simple, accurate and speedily operated information system will enable management to stay in real command of the business and to retain the initiative in decision-taking instead of being forced to react to crises. In many businesses this will mean reviewing sales and production levels daily, cash flow weekly, profitability monthly, stock levels and cost controls quarterly. Nothing should be left to six-monthly or annual audited accounts. Annual accounts are no more than an historical record of interest more to outsiders than to managers and they can form no part of any effective control system.

Finance

The possible sources of external finance have been outlined earlier. The important points for the business are to ensure that finance is made available in the correct total amount, in the various appropriate forms, from a number of different sources, and at appropriate cost. Each aspect merits separate consideration.

It is most important to estimate investment and working capital needs accurately in the initial stages and to ensure that an adequate margin for error is included. Nothing will be more damaging to the company's reputation with its finance sources than to seek to negotiate additional facilities unexpectedly at an early stage in operations. Indeed the loss of confidence caused may be so extreme as to prejudice existing facilities. Inexperience can sometimes lead to the entrepreneur asking for the absolute minimum amount needed due to a concern that to ask for more might produce a refusal. This concern arises from the assumption that a bank or investor will always wish to provide the minimum necessary. This is quite wrong. Most investors will be very glad to invest additional amounts in a proposal they like. Conversely, if they are not confident in the prospects offered by a proposal, they are most unlikely to be tempted into investing because the amount asked has been slightly reduced. Indeed, if their analysis of the cash requirements of the business plan shows a greater amount than that requested, this in itself may lead to a loss of confidence in the proposer's financial or business judgement with a consequent refusal.

The forms in which finance should be sought may well determine the sources from which it is sought. Generally speaking there is much to be said for placing the various forms of secured borrowing required with one source. It will simplify administration and may well reduce the overall costs without necessarily reducing the total amount available.

However, it would be unwise to rely entirely on one source for all forms of finance. No entrepreneur can be sure that his or her business will always be successful and that some form of crisis may not arise, temporary or otherwise. If all external finance is sourced from one institution then there is a risk that a loss of confidence by one party may be fatal to the business. In a crisis there will be great difficulty in securing additional finance rapidly from another institution which has no experience of dealing with the business in question. The fact that a crisis exists and that another bank or investor has refused to help may be enough to put off all new investors. By contrast, differing institutions may take good or bad views of a given situation. If a company has two or more sources of finance then it is more likely to be able to persuade one of them to take on a new liability or to substitute for an existing finance source in the event of difficulties. While it may be easier and less expensive to deal with only one institution in good times, it is well worth taking out 'insurance' against a crisis by having a number of separate lines of credit.

The forms and costs of finance are interrelated and will vary substantially for larger firms at different times in the business cycle. For the small firm, a choice may not be freely available. Equity shares in small firms are not freely market-able and can therefore only be sold to those who are willing to hold them for the medium or long term. The smaller and more remote the prospect of capital gain for the investing institution, the higher will be its required dividend yield and the greater its need for assurance that profits will be available from which to pay dividends. All these requirements work against the acceptability of making equity investments in small firms and add to the administrative cost disincentives already described of making and monitoring such investments. Nevertheless, small businesses will be well advised to make every effort to secure a minority equity investment from an outside institution. While the total costs of dividend payments may be higher than interest payments, this disadvantage is balanced by the fact that in unprofitable years a dividend need not be paid at all whereas interest bills are payable irrespective of profitability.

Proprietors who feel completely confident of their continuing ability to pay interest bills sometimes ask why they should 'give away' 20 per cent or 30 per cent of the shares in their business to an institution that 'only' provides a different form of money to a bank. The benefits which may not be apparent are twofold. If the business is to grow, then beyond a certain size it will find it impossible to continue to borrow additional money without an increase in its capital base. If that capital base comes only from retained profits after tax, growth will inevitably be slowed and may even come to a halt as additional working capital needs become more and more difficult to satisfy. Sale of a part of the equity will not only increase the capital base immediately, but the consequent faster rate of profit growth will, of itself, improve the capital base and the willingness of existing or new external investors to buy more shares at premium prices. Thus a virtuous circle is created from the proprietor's point of view. In a sense, the more shares that proprietors sell, the faster their profits and the value of their remaining shares will grow. The point is easily observed by looking at the shareholdings of the great 'tycoons' in their own businesses. People who began with a 100 per cent shareholding have ended up owning only perhaps 10 or 20 per cent, but they are still in effective control and with shares worth hundreds of times their original value.

Apart from the 'gearing' effect on share prices described above, many institutions investing in small firms provide the further benefits of a 'hands-on' investment philosophy, usually through nominating a part-time non-executive director to the firm. Such appointments emphasize and underline the commitment of the investor to the business and are intended to provide an invaluable source of dispassionate but supportive advice. Equally, they give the institution a greater insight into the quality of the business and will often increase its willingness to offer additional investment when needed.

Financial needs greater than £75,000–100,000 can generally be met by fully secured lending. However, some businesses turn either from choice or necessity to a method of fund raising other than selling equity shares. They borrow, usually from banks or asset finance companies, on the security of personal guarantee, often secured on personal assets. Great care should be taken when raising finance by this method either to limit the guarantee or to pledge only assets that the borrower is prepared to lose without suffering personal financial disaster. Company directors who give a personal guarantee that they cannot afford to meet from free assets have effectively given up the protection of limited liability status and increased their risks to those of a partner or sole trader who risks personal bankruptcy. Lenders may say that the guarantee is taken mainly to ensure the commitment of the borrower to the business. This argument should be treated with reserve. No entrepreneur starts a business without being fully committed to it in all meaningful respects. The giving of a guarantee in reality ensures a commitment to the lender rather than to the business.

The giving of a personal guarantee not only increases financial exposure in a failure but it can also work to increase the likelihood of failure. In a business crisis the financial pressure of a personal guarantee may distort business judgement at a time when it most needs to be clear and unemotional. Too many business people struggle on in a hopeless trading position in the hope rather than the expectation of protecting their guarantee. They usually end up causing additional losses both to themselves and to their creditors. Conversely, others who are more prudent, or perhaps more faint-hearted, close their businesses prematurely in order to be certain that they will not incur any liability under a guarantee that they have given. Neither type of reaction can be considered to be a good decision in a crisis.

Five tips for success

(1) Plan and run your business with the benefit of all available expert operational and financial advice.
(2) Create the broadest possible financial base for the business and ensure your personal financial exposure is limited and tolerable.
(3) Always base your plans and budgets on a thorough study of existing or new markets. Every business should be market-led and not product-driven.

(4) Aim for steady, profitable growth and ensure you create and develop the management team needed to handle expansion.

(5) Make sure you create and use those operational and financial controls which will enable you to make prompt and well-informed choices among available options.

6
Successful Businesses –
The High Technology View

Harry Nicholls
Managing Director and Chief Executive, Birmingham Technology Ltd,
Aston Science Park

Before taking up his present position as Managing Director and Chief Executive of Birmingham Technology Limited in December 1983, Harry Nicholls spent over 20 years as a business school academic and business adviser.

He became closely involved in 1981 (as a member of a working group drawn from Aston University, the City of Birmingham and Lloyds Bank plc) with the process of planning and developing a suitable organization to establish Aston Science Park.

Introduction

Birmingham Technology Limited (BTL), which runs Aston Science Park, is probably the science park management company most committed to the provision of management support to tenant companies in the UK. Birmingham Technology's explicit mission is the creation of wealth and employment in Birmingham through encouraging the establishment and promotion of rapid-growth, knowledge-based companies by the provision of business, management and technological support, venture funding and flexible accommodation to meet their changing requirements.

Birmingham Technology Limited realized there was a funding gap for small businesses. Despite exhortations from the financial community that there are plenty of funds but a shortage of good ideas expressed as business propositions, Birmingham Technology believed some high technology companies were facing problems with finance. They felt there was a lack of willingness by funding institutions to provide equity, rather than loan money, in amounts of less than £100,000. This lack of involvement was exacerbated by a reluctance to support high-tech start-ups requiring perhaps seven or eight years to reach a stage of company development which would allow investors to realize a return on their investment. Birmingham Technology decided to fill this gap by creating their own venture capital fund which is used to finance tenants at Aston Science Park.

When Birmingham Technology was established they believed it was probable that the managers of new high technology companies, while strong in technical expertise, were likely to have weaknesses in the areas of marketing, finance and operations management. They believed that new companies would almost certainly lack a balanced management team and might also lack an adequate understanding of their company's position in its market-place. The management team of Birmingham Technology therefore possesses a very wide range of business experience and expertise. The function of the team, in addition to the effective selection of those potential companies which are likely to benefit from, and contribute towards, the aims of the Park, is to provide ongoing support and assistance to the companies in Aston Science Park. The role is perhaps well described as that of the ultimate in teaching companies, or the application of action learning which leads to effective business management in new knowledge-based companies.

Experience is teaching that although the details of areas such as technology, markets, personnel and finance vary from company to company, there are a number of problems and opportunities which occur with some regularity. These are particularly evident among new business start-ups and companies whose activities are based on consultancy or software development. Some issues become apparent during the initial appraisal stage when companies are being considered for support and funding from Birmingham Technology. Other opportunities and problems only arise as the businesses begin to develop. These factors are reviewed in the remainder of this chapter.

High technology entrepreneurs

Very few high technology entrepreneurs are able to combine technological expertise with a good sense of business. The successful entrepreneur needs drive and ambition, technical expertise or competence, common sense and vision to see links between different aspects of any business or business opportunity. Technological entrepreneurs should be aware of the life cycle in new products. There is a need to develop new products as existing products come to the end of their life cycle. This will also need a particular business structure incorporating both research and development, sales and production.

Previous business experience can be very important. Two of the most successful companies at Aston Science Park were set up by groups of entrepreneurs who had previously been working in other companies. They knew each other as a team, they knew how each other worked, and they were all keen to have a go at developing a business for themselves rather than for somebody else.

Management teams

Many companies lack a balanced management team. Management teams of four or five are probably the optimum, the most successful management teams usually have a broad base of complementary experiences. Typically technologists come forward either straight from a technological background or from larger companies with technological experience and perhaps sometimes experience of a single area of management. Even when companies are set up by four or five people with considerable management expertise problems can arise. Many experienced entrepreneurs have big company perspectives; they have got used to the support offered by larger companies, such as purchasing, accounts, research and various other sorts of everyday help. When developing their own small business they often have to undertake these functions themselves.

Concept development and appraisal

The individual or team with a technical idea usually sees a product's technical advantages. Birmingham Technology, or other financial backers, who may become interested in a project are often more interested in evaluating the market for a particular technological idea or product. This is the first area with which Birmingham Technology find themselves having to assist companies. They frequently have to suggest that a basic but realistic market research exercise is undertaken. There is a need to understand the product, the requirements of the market and how the market can be developed to exploit their idea.

Care should be taken in selecting a market research company. It is relatively easy for market research companies to come up with a list of names of companies which would have an interest in the product. But the value of market research comes from knowing and understanding how the market operates. This is far more important than a list of names and addresses.

In developing a product there is a need to consider who will buy the product and how much they are willing to pay. Many technology-oriented entrepreneurs are keen to undertake extra development work to further refine the product. Market research should evaluate whether the extra development work will actually pay for itself in the market.

Companies should develop a business plan and know it inside out. It has to be *their* business plan. When Birmingham Technology look in their systematic way at business plans they go through them thoroughly looking for weaker points. This is exactly the same approach that should be taken by entrepreneurs or technologists (from a detached viewpoint) when looking at their own business plan. Any review of a business plan will involve asking questions. These questions are often simply ways of trying to 'get inside the business' and understand the idea and the entrepreneur. Birmingham Technology examine company business plans as the first stage of the appraisal process before deciding whether or not to accept companies onto the Science Park. At the appraisal stage they often find that the entrepreneur neither possesses nor can raise the required capital. This poses particular questions of capital structure when, as almost invariably happens, the entrepreneur is very reluctant to accept less than 76 per cent of the equity – indeed most would prefer to own over 90 per cent. It also leads to problems of evaluation of the time, effort and financial sacrifice which the entrepreneur has devoted to develop the business idea to the stage of an application to venture capitalists for the funds needed to establish the business on a larger scale – so-called 'sweat capital'.

Business plans

Companies need to put together their own business plans and have confidence in them. The company needs to have sufficient energy and commitment to take its business plan seriously. However, although considerable amounts of time and discussion will be spent on developing a business plan, it will rarely be fulfilled in its entirety. Flexibility should be built into business plans so that when crises are encountered appropriate action can be taken. Plans for the development of a business will rarely take place at the pace envisaged; development often takes place too quickly or too slowly.

In developing a business plan time needs to be spent in discussing the plan with as many other appropriate people as possible. Such people include business advisers, other businesses that have undertaken similar developments and other business people. Only by discussion and presenting your case to others will you know it thoroughly yourself. This process also allows the reappraisal of the idea. The entrepreneur will change his or her views of the business and the business plan will change. Changes in the business plan will also change the entrepreneur. These changes must take place together. The whole process of developing a business plan can be very long and arduous.

When most companies come to see Birmingham Technology their first business plans are very optimistic with a small loss in the first few years and then profits. Birmingham Technology evaluate the business plan and give a more realistic appraisal of development time and costs. Losses during the first few years are usually greater and profits are achieved at a later date. In reality, the business will usually encounter various crisis points during its development and losses may have to be endured longer even than Birmingham Technology envisage before profits are returned. Many companies fail to produce realistic business forecasts because they are unaware of the long lag in the decision-making process in large companies. Smaller businesses hoping to sell to large companies can face a two-year lag before sales can be accepted and agreed. This obviously slows down the development of sales to larger companies.

Business plans are equally important for developed companies. The business plan provides a disciplined path so that at the end of the year or reappraisal period, the company can see where it has strayed from that path. All companies should have a budget for the year and reappraisal of the business plan should also be undertaken. However, in later years once the business is established, they may have considerable problems in finding the time to review and prepare business plans. Growth in the company should allow these areas to be delegated to the management team, which hopefully will have been created by the growth in the company requiring more management expertise.

There is a need to strike the right balance between sticking to plans and adopting a flexible approach. Too much adhesion to business plans can promote 'paralysis by analysis' – too much analysis of a problem can make an entrepreneur scared of making a decision or not proceeding. The right balance is probably the company which looks back and says that it would not have started doing what it is doing now if it had known what it knows now. Companies therefore need drive and ambition, but also the flexibility for change.

There is a need for entrepreneurs to be able to take informed risks. However, realism and common sense are necessary. It is here that financial analysts frequently provide poor advice. Many analysts are used only to viewing companies as figures on a page. Some have little understanding of the risks which have been taken and hunches which have been pursued in order to arrive at a company's present or possible future trading position. There is a need to strike the right balance between being a risk-taker and someone who is rather intransigent to change and risks. Informed risk-taking is often necessary.

Advising businesses

Birmingham Technology sit on the sidelines and try to help companies achieve a balance between different functions, for example getting the balance right between areas of the company's activities or getting the right management team. However, there are key points in the development of any business when it is necessary to know when to put effort into a particular function. One example is shown by the consultancy companies at Aston. They generate very good cash flow but have relatively poor prospects of long-term growth. Some of these companies have had to be pushed into developing product ideas and foregoing current cash flow. As a result they encounter cash flow problems, but this may be what is needed at a particular time to enable the company to produce a product on which to build its future success.

At Aston a non-executive director is put on the board of all the companies. On some occasions non-executive directors take an active role in the company's operations. For some entrepreneurs the desire for independence is very strong and they do not take kindly to advice. It is usually best to give these companies advice by putting them into close contact with others who have suffered similar problems. Often telling them what needs to be done is not very well received. At Aston, with its very close-knit environment of high technology companies in close proximity, encountering similar problems, this is relatively easy. It is suggested that companies in a similar situation could develop this environment for themselves by joining business associations or undertaking discussions with other small businesses that have gone through similar problems.

At Aston marketing and finance consultancy companies have been accepted onto the Science Park so that they can provide formal and informal business help to the other companies on site. Good consultancy can be helpful to the development of some companies. Small companies do not have experience in all areas so it is essential in many cases to buy in this experience. Many people have mixed opinions and experiences of consultants; however, if a good consultant can be found he or she can often be very beneficial. Accountants are not always the best individuals to help with the development of a business. Their experience is often not broad enough to provide help in management advice.

Losing old habits

Many entrepreneurs first start trading from home. Habits or parsimony are built in. Spending is not something that they easily undertake; it often becomes very difficult for them to spend money. However, to promote a high technology image or to take on good-quality personnel requires money and spending. It costs money to hire good-quality people. Poor-quality people come far cheaper but are usually less effective; the same is often true of premises and the promotion of an image. Birmingham Technology often have to ask companies if they are spending enough. However, it is equally important to ensure that individuals do not take too much money out of the business too quickly. Every £1,000 extracted from a company in its formative years is £1,000 that might have been invested in the future growth of the company and therefore is £1,000 which might have accumulated considerably larger returns in the long run.

When companies are growing rapidly and sales are increasing, the company may be expanding beyond the levels outlined in a business plan. At this point it is necesssary for the business to spend in order to be prudent. If spending is only undertaken at the levels of growth envisaged in the business plan, the business may not be spending enough to allow its growth to proceed at the appropriate rate. Spending should be kept in line with the level of growth in the company. It is obviously necessary to spend more because more management time and resources are required to handle and undertake the extra business created by fast business growth.

Marketing

If a company does not market effectively, it will not get customers, it will not sell products and it will not be successful. In the formative years of a company it is crucial to have a knowledge and grasp of marketing. As the company develops and sales develop the key is often to have an effective sales team and a sales administrative section. This will require the recruitment of good-quality sales personnel. However, a note of caution should be raised here. One company at Aston which was recruiting a new salesperson had one outstanding candidate with considerable practical experience and academic qualifications. This person seemed the ideal candidate for the job. It was only on closer inspection that the company realized that the applicant came from one of their competitors. Previous experience at Aston has shown that one way in which competitors try to find out more about their opposition is to send along their own personnel for job interviews in competitors' companies. A considerable amount of information can be gleaned about a company's activities, markets and future plans during a job interview.

Start-up companies often need to penetrate the decision-making levels of larger companies to develop their sales. To do this requires somebody with a suitable level of expertise, experience and confidence. Senior personnel in large businesses need to 'identify' with their clients. Many small business founders do not have this experience. To be successful and generate sales to large customers it may therefore be necessary to take on somebody to perform this role. This can often be one of the hardest decisions for many small business entrepreneurs. To achieve sales to larger companies involves either taking on sales or marketing directors or, particularly in the early years, taking on a new managing director. The existing entrepreneur can then become the chairperson. However, this is a costly process and expenditure of about £30,000 per annum is required to take on the right person. In addition he or she may wish to take an equity stake in the business as well. This raises the dilemma for all entrepreneurs of having to rescind both their involvement and equity stake in a business. In most cases it is necessary to take on quality management in order to achieve growth. Continuing with the original entrepreneur may restrict company growth.

Most high technology companies have a tendency not to sell standard items. Their products have modifications or additional components. Companies selling standard products undertake standard production methods which often have some level of repetition and therefore can be costed at standard product prices. The addition of modifications, extra components or further work on any standard product involves considerable additional work, materials and time. This does not make it a standard product and it should not, therefore, be charged at standard product prices. Pricing policies should take account of these factors.

Many technologists see a technical problem as a challenge. They develop a product that will provide excellent results in particular areas — A, B and C. But when approaching customers they are more willing to consider adding on items or features D and E rather than just selling the basic product which provides A, B and C effectively. It is essential to sell what you have got and only then consider adding features and obviously asking extra for them. Technologists do not always appreciate this; the technological problem is often very attractive but not financially worth while.

Independence and staying small

The growth of a business, particularly in the high technology field, requires money. This requirement for money often involves equity being taken away from the entrepreneur, whose independence and control are thus diminished. Success, in the conventional sense, may therefore destroy the independence which some small businesses seek. Independence is essentially a good thing; it is a goal which many small business owners desire. However, if companies intend to stay small they should try to choose a market which allows them to remain small. Independent small businesses cannot really be developed in areas which are currently served by larger mass producers. To remain small and independent usually requires companies to undertake a considerable degree of specialization. However, it should be remembered that all small businesses should have a considerable commitment to their customers. Independence can therefore be illusory.

Five tips for success

(1) High technology entrepreneurs need to understand that technology is a means to an end. Developing new technology is very interesting but it will not usually 'pay for itself'. Entrepreneurs have to see technology as a means of making the company successful. They also need to have drive, ambition and a desire for success.
(2) The product needs to serve a market, and this market has to have the potential for growth.
(3) The entrepreneur has to be willing to take risks, but these risks should be tempered by an appreciation of the business and the market-place.
(4) Companies need to develop and understand their business plan, but flexibility is required because the world is not always the same as they thought it was or will be. Companies need to learn from their experience and be able to take good advice.
(5) It has to be accepted that as the company grows, the company will have to change. Growth will often necessitate the recruitment of new personnel and possibly the entrepreneur being placed on the sidelines.

7
Successful Businesses –
The Business Adviser's View

Peter Lovell
General Manager, London Enterprise Agency

Peter Lovell worked for a number of small businesses in the publishing, printing, building and import/export industries before joining Barclays Bank at the age of 25. He worked for Barclays for ten years, spending the last two on secondment to the London Enterprise Agency (LEntA) which he eventually joined on a permanent basis. His duties as general manager involved assisting in the development of small businesses. In 1987 he left LEntA to establish Barnet Enterprise Trust.

Introduction

The London Enterprise Agency (LEntA) and assistance to small businesses

Like all agencies making up the ever expanding network of support groups for small companies, the London Enterprise Agency (LEntA) comes into contact with a wide range of businesses, a diverse cross-section of people and widely differing views of success.

The London Enterprise Agency is one of the oldest and largest of the enterprise agencies currently operating in the United Kingdom. It was set up in 1979 by nine major companies which had a collective wish to see something done to assist job creation by helping people set up in business and by helping existing small companies to expand, and to relieve inner-city dereliction.

Since that time the corporate membership of LEntA has grown to seventeen (Arthur Andersen & Co., Barclays Bank PLC, The British Petroleum Co. PLC, Citibank NA, Investors in Industry PLC (3i), IBM United Kingdom Ltd, John

Laing PLC, Legal and General Group PLC, Lex Service PLC, Marks and Spencer PLC, Midland Bank PLC, Shell UK Limited, Tate & Lyle PLC, United Biscuits (UK) Ltd, The Wellcome Foundation Ltd and Whitbread & Company PLC) and the work undertaken by the Agency has increased many-fold.

The Agency's primary objectives are:

(1) To create viable jobs and economic growth through an expansion of small businesses in the capital.
(2) To enable the private sector both to work together and in partnership with the public sector and to tackle specific projects which aid inner-city regeneration.
(3) Where appropriate, to undertake innovative projects which can either be applied elsewhere in the UK or have a national benefit.

Although LEntA is a purely private-sector body it works with both central and local government and has set up joint projects with London boroughs, the Inner London Education Authority (ILEA) and various colleges and universities. It receives project funding from the Manpower Services Commission for training and from the Department of the Environment for inner-city projects.

The encouragement and growth of small firms are seen as LEntA's primary objectives. It is the belief of the sponsors that Inner London, with its mass of old buildings and its spending power, is particularly suited to the development of small businesses. Through its counselling services and its extensive range of small business training courses LEntA helps around 3,000 people each year to review their business ideas. The main purpose of both counselling and training is to help the entrepreneur (either intending or actual) to prepare a business plan with a strong emphasis on marketing and to identify the most appropriate source of funding.

Business advice: company strengths and weaknesses

In the course of its work, the Agency comes into contact with a range of businesses, each with their own strengths and weaknesses. It is appropriate to look at some of these problems and strengths to assess what can be learned from them.

Some five years ago, cash flow was the major difficulty for small businesses and firms would seek advice on how to overcome this problem. Many of these clients came to the Agency with very little experience of financial issues, and frequently with accounts which were years out of date.

The first indicator that the visitor would have had of a 'cash flow crisis' was the fact that the bank was bouncing cheques. There was very little that could be done to help save these companies, since bank support would not be forthcoming and investment (even if acceptable to the promoter of the business) unlikely to be made available in time.

Most of those firms are now gone. They were kept alive for a little longer than would have been the case because of Customs and Excise and Inland Revenue strikes, but when the authorities started to chase up the backload of unpaid taxes this was the last nail in their coffin. The survivors are, for the most part, much stronger and better managed. They will have a reasonable idea of their break-even, will watch their cash flow and will know their markets.

The new firms which have started up in the past few years (and most of the million-plus new jobs which have been created since 1979 are in firms employing 20 people or less), are more likely to have had the benefit of business training and have the opportunity to use the network of advice services that has sprung up in recent years.

Sharing success and growth

There has been a change in the British attitude to the acceptance of 'someone else in the business'. Some five years ago the 'Marriage Bureau', as LEntA's Business Introduction Service to link investors and small firms was then known, had difficulty finding business people who would accept equity-linked capital into their business. Entrepreneurs wanted to run the whole show and did not want the 'interference' of an investor, even if that investor could, as often happens, bring much more than money into the business.

A lot of this attitude sprang from the fact that it was so easy (at that time) to get borrowed money for a project under the government's Loan Guarantee Scheme. This route did not involve any sacrifice of independence. Since much of the research that has been undertaken on business start-up shows that most people go into business in order to achieve independence, perhaps that fact is hardly surprising.

Things have slowly changed over the past few years, and now the chief handicaps to the linking of potential investor and would-be investee are twofold: the cautiousness of the investor and the optimism of the promoter of the business. It is inevitable that investors are cautious. They are being asked to put a significant sum of capital into a company with no guarantee when that money will be repaid, if ever. The risks are high, but so are the rewards, in some cases. Investors will hope that the effort that they put into the firm, either on a part-time or full-time basis, will increase its chance of success. The LEntA service, which is now set up as an independent company called Local Investment Networking Company (LINC), specializes in the £20,000–50,000 area of investment.

The optimism of the promoter of the business is less easy to overcome, but overcome it must be if investment is to be obtained. The major problem is that this optimism leads entrepreneurs to overvalue their business, sometimes by a very great deal. It is not unusual to sit across the table from someone looking for investment, where a balance sheet shows the company to be insolvent, on any objective assessment. The profit and loss account shows that perhaps the firm is now breaking even or making a small profit. Software companies are probably the worst. The product is usually '90 per cent' developed, and the business person is typically looking for £20,000 to complete the development and market the product. The developer has ignored two factors: first, that the last 10 per cent of any programme is the most difficult part, and second that there are already many, many software packages on the market. Why should theirs sell?

One company where LEntA was successful in introducing investor to investee was in the computer field, though not in writing programs. The company concerned was involved in staff recruitment in programming and related fields. The company's balance sheet was nothing to write home about. Losses had been incurred as a result of the activities of a third director who had since left, leaving a situation where the company was, technically at least, insolvent. The company made a pitch at one of LEntA's 'investors' meetings', where those looking for capital make a presentation to an audience of potential investors. These meetings are particularly interesting, since companies looking for cash are encouraged to make their presentations as 'visual' as possible, making use, where appropriate, of flip-charts, slides and videos, and demonstrating their product where there is one. Small fashion shows have even been staged, where the seeker of capital has been running a fashion design company. The advantage of such meetings is that 'the dog can see the rabbit' and vice versa. There is no mileage, for an entrepreneur, in becoming involved with an investor with whom day-to-day relations are going to be difficult. The converse is, of course, equally true.

At the investors' meeting the computer recruitment firm met a businessman of immense experience who had recently returned to the UK from the Far East. He put £10,000 into the company to secure its future. He also agreed to work for the firm on a part-time basis, probably about two days a week. Soon, however, this involvement became full-time, and the company has prospered to such an extent that they have now joined the Business Introduction Service again, this time as a potential investor.

That company has done well, thanks to the additional capital and management expertise that were introduced and to a lot of hard graft from all concerned. It is interesting to see how, over the three or four years, their goals have changed. Initially the remaining two original directors were keen, hard working and dedicated, but they were concerned solely with survival. Prospects were good, but the immediate outlook was bleak, and the main goal was to earn enough to pay expenses as they fell due.

With success has come a new goal – to be more successful. For most entrepreneurs, money in itself is not of paramount importance, but in a capitalist society it is the only yardstick of success. This wealth is quite often accumulated inside the business itself and it is often difficult for any significant part of it to be withdrawn unless an outright sale of the company is undertaken. This is seldom an option to be contemplated. Even when the dizzy heights of a Stock Exchange listing are achieved, when the entrepreneur is, on paper at least, a millionaire, few make large-scale adaptations to their lifestyle. This would involve selling precious shares!

Alternative criteria for success

Many of LEntA's best clients have as their goal the simple wish to do things well, to be the best in their field. One company, for example, was proud that they made the most expensive snooker cues in the world and that they had a six-month waiting list! Their goal was to make the best, and they had achieved it, the evidence being that their products were being used by top professionals all over the world.

Coupled with the goal of job satisfaction, is that of what the sociologists call 'peer-group recognition'. This goal has always been to the fore in most of the many clients in the fashion trade. To many fashion designers money is of no importance at all, and this is proved by the fact that most of them could earn more working for someone else, be it within the fashion industry or outside it. The important thing is to see their garments paraded up and down a catwalk and to hear favourable things said about them. As can be imagined, this is not always the most satisfactory base for starting a business that will survive, let alone expand. The business is often faced with the task of trying to inject some realism (particularly of a financial nature) into their ideas. Sometimes that is possible, sometimes not. The most successful fashion designer client to date is unusual in that she combines superb talents for designing for the market-place with great entrepreneurial skill. She is, quite simply, one of the most astute business people in fashion or in any other field. She also possesses one enormous additional talent: she listens to advice.

Few entrepreneurs would claim that their goal when they went into business was to create jobs, but once staff are employed there is often a fierce loyalty towards staff who prove to be satisfactory. It must be admitted, though, that this is often coupled with a ruthless determination to deal summarily with those who prove to be less so, especially where dishonesty is suspected. One client, an upholstery firm in Bermondsey, was started four years ago by two girls who are now in their mid-twenties, and now employs seven staff, two of them on the Youth Training Scheme (YTS), and one young man who was taken on via YTS and has been kept on. The business has had its bad times, but the people running the firm refused to take the easy way out and lay off staff, not out of sentimentality, but because to do so would see the results of their training programme dissipated. As things improved, they were proved right.

Markets, ambitions and independence

The London Enterprise Agency has paid particular attention to developing new markets for small businesses. It has organized a number of events or activities such as 'Meet the buyers' where purchasing managers from large organizations explain how and what they buy, and two 'Can you make it?' exhibitions. These events, which were organized in conjunction with the Confederation of British Industry (CBI), allowed fifty large companies to exhibit products and components which they were importing, to enable the small firm audience to have a chance to provide an alternative quotation.

Although LEntA seeks no special favours for its small firm clients, buyers from sponsor companies and from major retailers spend time speaking and counselling on LEntA courses, to train small firms on how to sell. A more sophisticated variation of this is the 'Profit in store' exhibition where small firms supplying consumer products meet buyers from UK and North American department stores.

It is always especially satisfying when the goals of clients include a wish to export. When clients start work on a business plan they are always asked to include in it an 'objectives' page, broken down into short-term intentions (the next six months), medium-term aims (six months to two years) and long-term ambitions (two to five years). Normally one would expect to see a desire to export under at least one of these headings, unless the business is obviously inappropriate. This is not merely for reasons of personal patriotism (though there is an element of that motivation involved) but because often such an objective indicates that the client has decided that, sooner or later, his or her market has to be larger than the United Kingdom.

Having mentioned the objectives page of the business plan, perhaps it is pertinent to mention the difference between 'objectives' or 'goals' and ambitions. The big question here is: 'If you are starting out in business should you have big ambitions, or limited ambitions?' The 'correct' answer, as most readers will by now have probably guessed, is big ambitions. Objectives should be realistic and goals attainable, but never, never limit your ambitions. The argument is not one of mere semantics, it is very real and very important. While business goals should be something to strive for and, if possible, attain, entrepreneurial ambitions can never be fully realized, nor should they be.

Great ambitions, on their own, do not of course lead to the foundation of a successful business. Is there a common thread which runs through the successful businesses which sets them apart, makes them instantly recognizable, which points to lessons that others might learn? It is often said that one of the great advantages that the small firm has over the large corporation is flexibility. Comparisons are often made to the small speedboat and the ocean liner. There is certainly much truth in this, but until the nation revises its attitude to failure, it will not exploit this advantage to the full.

It is true that the small company can often change direction very quickly when it needs to, and that often change will be in time to avert disaster. Frequently, however, despite that quality of flexibility the redirection of activity will come too late, and the company will fail. In the United Kingdom such failure is accompanied by stigma both during and after, often long after, it occurs. The Americans have a much healthier attitude to 'failure'. They will regard the fact that an entrepreneur has failed before (provided that it is not a habitual practice) as being a sign not of weakness, but of strength. They believe that lessons will have been learned in the failure that will not be repeated in the new enterprise.

Most entrepreneurs cherish the idea of independence. Most show a willingness, sometimes almost a desire, to work long, lonely hours for little reward, with no certainty that it will all work out in the end. That love of independence is a weakness as well as a strength. Independence can sometimes mean a reluctance, sometimes a total resistance, to sacrifice any part of the business in order to take it forward. This is a great pity, but attitudes are slowly changing. Perhaps part of the clue lies in that description 'sacrificing', as though it were all take and no give. The truth is that raising money in the form of investment rather than by borrowing can mean that the small firm can become larger much more quickly. If the investment is accompanied by management expertise (in the form of a non-executive director appointed by a venture capitalist, or the direct involvement of the investor) then the investee company gains twice over.

Many of the investors registered with LEntA's LINC scheme are private individuals almost all of whom want to be involved in the businesses into which they are investing. LINC tries to match skills as well as money. Where a sales-oriented company is looking for cash but lacks good financial management it is suggested that they look for an investor who can provide the missing skills. Those who accept that such an arrangement is worth investigating are, almost by definition, more likely to succeed than those who do not.

While explaining the advantages of taking investment as opposed to borrowing when this seems to be appropriate, it is not LEntA's practice to sell venture capital. The simple question is posed: 'Would you rather have 70 per cent of a successful, adequately financed and well-managed company, or 100 per cent of a struggling one?' The initiative has to come from the entrepreneur, otherwise the sale of shares will always be a much-resented sacrifice.

Business skills and success

A common attribute of a successful business is that partners or directors possess different skills, different likes and dislikes, and even different attitudes. Too often people will go into business with a partner who is exactly like themselves. The end result is that both of them will either love or hate selling, both of them will or will not do the books, and both of them will be delegating or failing to delegate to staff. Successful partnerships usually comprise people who are very different. One will be quiet, charming and eager to oblige, the other tough, determined and probably quite arrogant. One will deal with customer complaints, smooth the ruffled feathers of staff and put off pressing creditors, the other will chase up late deliveries of raw materials, ruffle the feathers of staff when necessary and chase errant debtors. One will hire, the other will fire. One will probably sell, the other will probably buy. They both know what the other is doing, however, and are working to a common aim.

Innovation and business development

Some of the successful businesses which LEntA has advised have been product based, usually attempting to exploit an innovation or a new design concept. A common criticism levelled against banks and venture capitalists in the UK is that they will not back such inventive entrepreneurs. While the UK possesses some of the greatest inventors in the world, the argument runs, those inventors cannot get the backing that they need here and so the idea is developed by competitors abroad. There was undoubtedly a great deal of truth in this argument in the past, and there probably remains some substance to it even today. Much has been done to help the inventor by the development of science parks and similar institutions, including the 'Science City' development near London's Elephant and Castle, which does magnificent work in helping high-tech companies to set up and expand. Many inventors, however, lack the essential business skills to develop their ideas, and are reluctant to surrender their ideas to others. For the realistic ones, however, the future is brighter than it has ever been, and the chances of success greater.

Five tips for success

From the many firms which LEntA has advised an examination of their subsequent development identifies five key themes or 'tips for success'. While each business will have its own idiosyncratic approaches to success, there are common themes worth passing on to others thinking of starting up or developing their business.

(1) Know the break-even point for the business. This is the one indicator which can turn triumph to disaster, or vice versa. Significantly, it is the one indicator that was found to be most commonly known among borrowers under the government Loan Guarantee Scheme.

(2) Do not confuse profit and cash (or vice versa). Cash does not necessarily mean profit, and profit does not necessarily mean cash. Most businesses would be wise to acknowledge this before they start to produce both profit forecasts (or budgets), as well as cash flow forecasts. Proprietors of small firms would also be sensible to monitor regularly actual results against their forecasts, so that immediate corrective action can be taken.

(3) Be wary of the 'big order'. Many firms come unstuck by accepting an order which is too large for their production capacity, for their finances, or for their management to handle. The big order can be a godsend, provided that delivery dates can be met, payment terms are satisfactory and the acceptor is not putting all its eggs into one basket. It can also be potentially disastrous if the implications of accepting it are not carefully considered.

(4) Be proud of the company. Lack of pride and confidence will soon communicate itself to staff and customers alike, and can only lead to eventual failure.

(5) Be lucky!

8
A Financially Successful Company:

Kwik-Fit

Although no longer small, in the usual sense of the word, Kwik-Fit organizes its operations on the basis of a number of small depots. The company provides a fine example of a financially successful business. It was started in 1971 and has expanded rapidly. It currently operates 374 specialist repair and tyre and exhaust centres throughout the UK and has a workforce of 2,348 employees. The company has been developed under the personal supervision of Chairman and Chief Executive, Tom Farmer. Turnover of the business has increased rapidly in recent years from £43.3m in 1983 to £125.5m in 1987 with pre-tax profits showing similar rises from £2.6m in 1983 to £16.0m in 1987. The group also operates in The Netherlands and Belgium both as Kwik-Fit, with 60 depots, and USN, a distribution subsidiary, and in France through 41 centres. The group's philosophy is that of 100 per cent customer satisfaction and future market expansion is based on sound retailing principles.

Background

Although Kwik-Fit is not a one-man company its approach and style are the result of the current Chairman and Chief Executive, Tom Farmer. His is a classic growth story fuelled by his never-ending enthusiasm, motivation and ability to motivate others. Brought up in Edinburgh, he left school at 14 to help the family income. He is one of seven children. His first experience of business was as a 14-year-old advertising his services as a cooker cleaner. In 1956 he joined Tyre Scotland as a stores boy and earned £2 per week. He worked hard and by 18 was driving a van collecting old tyres. In 1961 he was poached by Tyre Services as a representative. Three years later, after a disagreement on bonuses, he left and rented a corner shop in Buccleuch Street in Edinburgh for £5 per week. With capital of £200 Tom Farmer was in business on his own, selling tyres. Early in the life of Tyre and Accessory Supplies, the name of the new Farmer company, he was fortunate to get free advertising in the form of an article about his 'cut price' operation. Tom relates how when he turned up at the shop on the morning the article appeared, 45 cars were waiting, nose to tail. The tyre business took off from then and Tom Farmer has not looked back since.

At this time the company consisted of Tom Farmer and two colleagues; each earned £12 and 10 shillings a week. The business soon expanded with the opening of four depots. New tyre legislation helped considerably as people were anxious to replace illegal tyres. Business was brisk and tyres were in short supply.

The takeover by Albany Tyre Services, a London-based, public-quoted company with 17 depots, was a major landmark in the development of the business. The folklore of this takeover is fascinating. The sale was concluded at a price of £450,000 and Farmer became a director and major shareholder managing the northern area. Farmer worked well with Stenson and Knight, the Albany directors. They were expansionist in their outlook and were constantly on the look-out for new acquisitions. Early attempts included Halfords and Standard Tyre. In 1971 they made a successful bid for Brown Brothers. This was another major turning point.

Brown Brothers was a large company, three times the size of Albany Tyres. The sheer size and management structure were not attractive to Farmer. Even as third largest shareholder and with promises of becoming chairman he resigned and announced that he had retired. At 29, with £1 million he and his family took an extended holiday in the United States. Always thirsty for new ventures much of the time in the USA was spent looking at new market opportunities. Tyres were no longer as attractive because the radial had extended the replacement period significantly. The American 'muffler' centres, however, were an attractive idea. Exhaust systems will always wear out, most then only lasted between 18 months and 2 years.

Developing Kwik-Fit

Back in Scotland, Farmer rounded up ten or so of his early staff and set up an exhaust fitting station. He was moving from a business which he understood well, in which five tyres fitted 80 per cent of the market, into unknown territory in which almost every make and model of car were different. In 1974, three years after forming Kwik-Fit, he sold the company to G.A. Robinson, a public company, for £700,000. The three-day week brought problems for Robinson; Farmer acquired a major shareholding in the company and started a rationalisation programme, disposing of most of its assets with the exception of Kwik-Fit and the Dutch Group Van Roy Dorsman. Farmer now had a substantial stake in a public company which, with the acquisition of the Euro Exhaust Centres in 1980 for £10m, expanded to 112 outlets.

Firestone was the next name to be associated with Kwik-Fit. Farmer heard that they were pulling out of Britain and quickly snapped up their 172 depots for £3.25m. Subsequently he sold half of the sites to Dunlop for the same £3.25m. The Firestone deal did, though, bring problems. Not all the depots were performing well; some of them were suffering due to bad management and procedures. Managing this level of expansion was more than the then Kwik-Fit management structure could cope with and at the same time maintain levels of profitability. Kwik-Fit profits fell from £4m to £1.6m.

Computers and management information

The control problem was solved by the installation of computer terminals in each depot. The computer project was led by one of Kwik-Fit's non-executive directors, John Padget. Tom Farmer readily acknowledged that none of the operational management were computer experts. Padget recommended an American company which had already been involved directly in computer applications in the retail trade. Early in 1982 200 terminals were installed in the depots. The installation took place on the same day and since then the company has not looked back. Staff were remarkably receptive to the computerization. The word 'computer' is not used in the company. The terminals are referred to as MATs — 'management action terminals'. Designed appropriately for non-office fingers, the system has run almost without problem. What is has done for Kwik-Fit is to give an almost continuous management information service linking together all the depots. Each evening, data from all depots, articles sold, prices and turnover and profits, is polled by central support office, Edinburgh. Each morning, management can see at a glance the performance of the entire organization. The system has now widened to minimize delays and paperwork and maximize efficiency. The system is linked to the major suppliers, for example, who can provide a 48-hour delivery service for stock items. Similarly prompt payment of invoices, on issue — which is very important to Tom Farmer — is made by computer saving the unnecessary delays and hassles of manual invoicing. The major credit card companies, Access and Visa, are now also linked up to the Kwik-Fit system giving almost instantaneous payment of credit card transactions, which form an increasingly important part of revenue.

Computers have also had an important part to play in terms of the personnel involved in the business. They have reduced the administrative staff required to manage the 374 depots from 100 to around 35. With this reduction also goes far tighter and more responsive management control. The MATs have also changed the role of the depot manager from administrator to 'doer'.

The initial expenditure on installation of the computers was approximately

£1m, although the company has subsequently invested more than £3m in additional equipment and software.

Management and staffing

The company is currently managed from head office in Edinburgh, below which there are five divisions – Scottish, Western, Eastern, Southern and London. Each division is controlled by a divisional director and a small management team responsible for sales, personnel, training, property and administration. Divisional offices are linked to Edinburgh by computer. Recently, warehouses have been added at divisional level for holding bulk purchases of tyres. The Kwik-Fit partner is the next in the hierarchy controlling three depots, while the Kwik-Fit Master manager is in charge of the individual depot.

At the top, the organization is extremely lean. Total administrative staff handling everything from salaries to stock orders is 35 people. In addition there are eight senior management positions: marketing and advertising director, sales director, finance director, customer services manager, new products and business development manager, property manager, computer manager and personnel and training manager. Three of these directors – sales, finance and commercial, dealing with administrative procedures and systems – report directly to Tom Farmer. The European operations each have a director who reports directly as well.

At the other end of the scale a hierarchy exists in the various grades of fitter. Farmer is convinced that everyone needs something to strive for and achieve. The fitters are divided into four categories: one-, two-, three- and four-star fitters. Promotion comes within the company so that everyone has a chance to improve his or her position and career prospects.

Senior management does not occupy a rarified position in the company. Tom Farmer himself is continuously involved in visiting the depots to maintain contact and motivate his workpeople to achieve greater things. One key element of this strategy for commitment is the profit share scheme introduced in 1986. This scheme is open to all workers who have been with the company for more than one month. It provides a real incentive to all staff. Equally important is the encouragement to increase profits. Frequent reminders are sent to depots to reduce waste and hence lower costs. One example of cost saving was the reduction in the company's electricity bill by £200,000.

Training, staff development and motivation

The company is committed to training of its staff at all levels, and sees training as a key element in its development. The company operates training and development centres in Edinburgh and Newcastle-under-Lyme. Courses are provided for all members of staff. All aspects of the business are covered including technical and product knowledge, depot management, sales techniques and communication skills.

The training programme has recently been revised and developed in modular form so that different modules can be taken as the employee develops through the company. Continuous assessment is made of each employee as he or she passes through the system so that senior management can monitor progress with a view to further development and promotion. In this way management information about performance can be kept. As in all aspects of the business reward is important; after each training module the employee is given a passport and certificate to indicate successful completion. The company is also involved in the Youth Training Scheme and has over 140 trainees at any one time working within the company. All YTS trainees are sent on a 12-week residential course in Livingston, Scotland. The course is run in conjunction with the Road Transport Industry Training Board. Part of the course include a week at the Loch Eil Outward Bound Centre in the Highlands. Like all aspects of training in Kwik-Fit, it is not an easy option. A tough regime is the rule rather than the exception.

Constant communication with staff reinforces the training programme and is designed to maintain 100 per cent commitment of staff to the company. The company produces a weekly newspaper, *Kwik-News*, as part of this communication drive. Each year, Kwik-Fit dances are held on six weekends so that all staff and their partners have the chance to meet their Chairman and Chief Executive. Tom Farmer insists on keeping in contact with employees. For managers, partners, suppliers and support staff the company holds an annual group sales conference. The event gets together all those involved directly or indirectly with the company to hear about and discuss current and future activity. Tom Farmer loves these types of occasion; they give him chance to show off his company and to enthuse the gathered assembly about its future.

Marketing and customer satisfaction

Like all well-managed retail businesses, Kwik-Fit is very conscious of its relations with customers. It strives for 100 per cent customer satisfaction. In all the literature it sends out to employees, customer relations are emphasized. Kwik-Fit argues that it is the best and is committed to maintain that position. Kwik-Fit subdivides its market into three broad categories and aims different parts of the business to each. Careful market analysis of these categories allows products to be targeted carefully. The first category is the 'price doesn't matter' group, about 20 per cent of the total. This group is made up mostly of business drivers, for whom convenience is the key element of the service. The Kwik-Fit fleet marketing development is aimed at this group. The second category, and the largest, representing some 60 per cent of customers, is labelled 'price and guarantee conscious'. These people own their cars and they represent a major investment to them. They want to see their vehicle maintained to a good standard and are willing to pay a fair price. The third category, 'price does matter', comprises those who are probably at the margins of car ownership and cannot afford high prices for products and guarantees. The 'budget' depots, of which there are 27, are aimed at this group.

The detailed approach to market analysis extends to broader analysis of the customers' attitude towards car repairs and servicing. Farmer argues that the repair business is traditionally an uncertain area for most people, a little like going to the doctor. Communication is all-important and the company has procedures to encourage positive communications between fitter and customer. Farmer's philosophy is clear: be honest and straightforward with the customer. If one is unsure about a problem, say so. At the beginning of each job discuss the problem with the customer. At the end, show the customer what has been undertaken.

This zeal for customer satisfaction is illustrated in the company response to complaints which arose as a result of a *Which* survey of car servicing. Immediately after the complaint, which the company accepted as quite justified and was caused by the work of one less than conscientious fitter, Tom Farmer issued a four-page response, mailed to the homes of each employee and also to the press. The response itemized all the elements of the complaint and in no uncertain terms reminded each employee of his or her responsibility to the company. Rather than take issue with the complaint Farmer simply demonstrated that if the Kwik-Fit codes of practice had been followed by the fitter, the situation would not have arisen.

Communication with the customer is a key element of the development strategy. While the company is national in scale, Farmer recognizes that a major concern of the motorist in the replacement market is that they like the 'small local garage' approach. While the Kwik-Fit national image is important, the 'small local garage' feel is vital. The company can then benefit from economies of scale in purchasing and advertising; there are few small competitors who could produce and screen the 'Kwik-Fit fitter' jingle, while at the same time maintaining a 'local' link. The current advertising budget is in excess of £9m. It is this local link which leads Farmer and the company to place so much emphasis on the individual depot and team of fitters.

Company growth and expansion

Looking forward there are several opportunities which Tom Farmer is considering. The company is currently looking at the car repair and service business as a whole. Recently it introduced the Kwik-Lube engine oil and filter service via a link-up with Mobil Oil. Turnover will soon be of the order of 5m litres of oil per year. They are further looking to segment the repair business and are looking at the possibility of opening some 100 new and much larger centres with bays specializing in all aspects of the car business – engines in bay 1, clutches in bay 2, brakes in bay 3. These units will be large, some 1,400 m^2 and located only in the major cities. At the other end of the scale there is also the opportunity to open up small units, 185 m^2 or so, simply for lubrication.

Geographically, most of the new market opportunities are in London and the South-east as this is the area of greatest concentration of cars, people and money. But in its assessment of the market Kwik-Fit realizes that a different strategy is required. While customers will travel some distance to a centre in the North and Scotland, congestion and travel times in the South-east require a much denser network of depots. The company retains a consultancy to search for new sites for the Kwik-Fit operation and is anxious to identify suitable locations, particularly in the London area.

Kwik-Fits's attributes

What, then, are Tom Farmer's views on successful business? Enthusiasm and energy are the most important elements. These come from the top down and affect everyone working in the organization. Tom Farmer recognizes the need to lead by example and to show all his employees the energy which is needed for the business to grow. Those with enthusiasm and energy make particularly successful managers and develop successful depots.

The ability to encourage staff to increase their own motivational levels depends partly on enthusiasm and partly on policy. Policies and mechanisms for staff motivation are vital to success. At Kwik-Fit all staff are encouraged to share in the success of the company through both the profit share scheme and the promotion possibilities which accrue from personal success. Kwik-Fit feels that employees respond to this and contribute individually to the overall performance of the business.

Commitment from all staff is also vital. This is perhaps most important at a senior management level in the organization. In Tom Farmer's case, Kwik-Fit is part of his family. They eat, drink and sleep Kwik-Fit. He expects and gets similar commitment from his senior staff. Commitment is also towards the customer. The '100 per cent customer satisfaction' slogan of the company and the 'You can't get better than a Kwik-Fit fitter' jingle is based on a complete belief in the company and commitment to perfection. These personal and attitudinal characteristics are followed by more traditional views of success.

Knowing the market and changes in market demands is taken for granted by Tom Farmer as an attribute for success. It is, though, something which Kwik-Fit has taken very seriously and has monitored carefully. The expansion of the company at present is based on very careful market analysis, recognition of developing opportunities and an understanding of the company's capabilities, strengths and weaknesses.

All new developments are based on careful planning. Tom Farmer stresses this in all his discussions. When the company enters new areas and products it is based on careful forecasting and planning. However, Tom Farmer's explanation of the initial failure in the French market is based on inadequate understanding of the market. This lack is no longer found in the Kwik-Fit organization.

Management control is the last key to Kwik-Fit success. Tom Farmer sees this as important to all retail organizations. This control has been built on the back of heavy investment in computerization and a belief in the importance of computers and the up-to-the-minute management information which they can provide. To the outsider, the use of management information systems and the commitment of the Chairman and Chief Executive to these systems epitomize the success of Kwik-Fit.

Tom Farmer's five tips for success

(1) Policies and mechanisms to encourage staff to motivate themselves, and to create enthusiasm are vital to success.
(2) Commitment from all staff is vital, and a 'can do' attitude is important at all staff levels.
(3) Knowing the market and changes in market demand is essential, linked with a 'no-nonsense' customer service.
(4) Decisions to enter new markets and develop new products need to be based on careful forecasting and planning.
(5) Management control is important, particularly in retail organizations. Computerization for control systems and the provision of up-to-the-minute management information are beneficial.

9
A Successful
High Technology Company:

Plasma Technology (UK) Ltd

Plasma Technology (UK) Ltd was started by David Carr and John Ball in 1981. Their company manufactures research equipment for producing silicon chips. By 1986 the company had increased its turnover to £5.5 million, it employed approximately 65 people and had pre-tax profits of over £1 million. It was at this point that the company considered entering the Unlisted Securities Market. However, they received two offers to purchase the business and eventually joined the Oxford Instruments Group. Both the founders have remained with the business and its growth has continued.

Background

Before starting Plasma Technology in 1981 David Carr and John Ball were working for a medium-sized high technology company in the South-west of England. Both were dissatisfied with their jobs and decided to leave the company. They left at different times but met soon afterwards to discuss the possibilities of starting their own business. They realized that they worked well together and had a useful blend of complementary skills. David Carr's experience was in sales and management and John Ball had technical and electronic expertise. From the very start of their discussions they realized they had to identify a market niche and develop a business to serve the gap they identified in their chosen market.

They concentrated their attention on developments in the microprocessor chip market, in particular in the equipment necessary to produce microchips. These chips are produced by coating a base material, usually silicon, with very thin layers of material. These build up to make layer upon layer of electrical circuitry. Two methods are usually used to do this – etching into the surface of the chip or depositing material onto the surface. Both processes use electrically energized chemically active gases (the gases are called plasma) to etch the surface or deposit materials. In 1981 this type of equipment could not be bought for less than £100,000 and only the largest public and private research organizations could afford this level of expenditure. The founders knew that microprocessor chip technology was making considerable advances and a lot of research was being undertaken in the field. Therefore, they decided to try and develop cheaper plasma etching equipment which could be more generally available to universities and the research laboratories of electrical companies.

Developing a business plan

Having identified a market niche David and John embarked on a very intensive period of market research and product development to investigate whether their idea was a viable basis for a business. These activities contributed to the development of a business plan for their company. The pair pooled their savings and for six weeks they worked intensively to investigate whether their idea was viable. John Ball developed prototypes, constantly refining the design to improve the performance and reduce the costs of the machine. David Carr used his marketing experience to investigate the market. He developed a list of all their potential customers in both the UK and abroad. He tried to estimate the number of machines each customer might want so that a clear estimate of the total target market could be obtained. A list of all companies throughout the world in a similar product area to theirs was developed to assess the intensity of the competition. They found only four or five major competitors worldwide.

Together they drew up a list of the strengths and weaknesses of the company. They attended trade and business exhibitions to improve and refine further their understanding of the market and to discuss their ideas with others. Throughout these discussions they were careful to ensure that people knew they had left their previous company and were working alone. They believed this was essential because they knew that in their industry some people could build a bad reputation for themselves if they developed their own business while working for another company or having access to inside information about competitors or customers. Trading in the formative years for these individuals who have generated a dishonourable reputation can be difficult since many companies do not want to be associated with them.

The end result of their market research and prototype development work was the production of a very detailed business plan for a machine which cost only £20,000, almost one-fifth of their competitors' machines. Individual components of the machine were carefully costed, production techniques were described and costed in detail, potential customers and sales figures were generated and trading figures for the first two years of the business were calculated. Their forecast suggested a turnover of £97,000 and £260,000 in the first and second year's trading respectively. In the event both these estimates were exceeded. Turnover in the first year was £115,000, 19 per cent above expectations. Second-year turnover was £700,000, more than two and a half times greater than expected.

Both founders firmly believe that their company's success was very reliant on the market research and development work undertaken to produce the business plan. Indeed, they blamed the inaccuracy of their forecasts and phenomenal early growth on the business plan's thoroughness. Little extra design or development work was needed to improve the product and they possessed a ready-made list of potential customers who were keener than expected to purchase their machine. They believe other companies which do not start with such a complete business plan may be slowed down in their early years by trying to start their business, develop the product and find new customers all at the same time.

Early company development

Having developed a business plan and confirmed in their own minds that the idea was viable, David and John decided to go ahead and develop their business. They pooled the remainder of their savings, remortgaged their houses and approached the major high-street banks for additional finance. The bank managers they approached were impressed by their business plan, financial commitment and experience and the third bank they visited granted them a modest £50,000 overdraft. Although the company was adequately financed in its early development stage the founders were always aware that the majority of the money they spent had come directly from 'their own pockets'. This instilled a strong commitment to obtaining value for money and prudent spending. Their experience has shown that this is not always the case with companies which receive large amounts of equity or venture capital when they start. Both founders believe many companies funded in this way are eager to purchase company cars, unnecessary machinery, expensive premises and office equipment. Plasma Technology was prudent in its early years. There was tight budgetary control and money was only spent as it was generated. The founders suggest that companies which finance their own development in this way will find it hard to get into financial difficulties, whereas venture capital-funded companies which have an early 'spending spree' often find it difficult to achieve a sufficiently high trading level in their formative years to cover these costs.

The company's rapid success, achieving sales of £700,000 in their second year, meant that they soon had to return to their bank manager for additional funds to finance the continued development of the business. It was at this point that they overcame a problem which they believed was one of the key turning points in the development of their business. To their surprise the bank manager, who had given a £50,000 overdraft to a business with no track record but a good business plan, was not willing to extend their overdraft limit 18 months later to a company with an impressive track record and high level of profits. David Carr suggests that this is not an unusual problem because bank managers are viewed favourably by their superiors for lending to new business customers, but they receive no additional recognition for lending additional funds to existing borrowers. Indeed, he suggests some managers get censured for taking addition-al risks and 'overexposing' the bank's position. As a result Plasma Technology successfully approached another bank for additional funds and transferred their account. As the company grew exactly the same problem occurred on two other occasions. The solution both times was the same. In total, the company has now changed banks three times.

As well as raising discontent over the attitude of some bank managers to assisting the early development of his business, David Carr is also critical of some of the other advisers assisting the development of small businesses. From his own experience and discussions with other entrepreneurs he believes that often the person or people best placed to deal with a business's problems are those involved in its development. He believes entrepreneurs will have analysed a problem and thought about any problems more carefully than any adviser. He has come across a number of examples of businesses facing a problem who approached advisers (both consultants and agencies) for help and were given off-hand, incorrect or faulty advice. He believes this is because many advisers do not have practical experience in running a small business. David Carr is now cautious of business advisers' help and believes many businesses could be successful if they had more confidence in their own judgement.

During the early development of the company both founders worked ex-tremely hard to establish the business. In the first two years they rarely worked less than a 12-hour day and a 6-day week. They often worked 24 hours a day to meet delivery deadlines. Since both founders are married with children this level of activity meant that they saw very little of their families during the formative years of the business. The support of their families to start the business and their continued support and understanding during its early years were, therefore, very important features. This is an important consideration which both founders were not fully aware of when they started the business. Indeed the lack of time they were able to spend with the younger children as they grew up is probably the only regret which they have about starting in business. However, both have the compensation of knowing that the success of their business has assured the future well-being of their families.

Company development and management

In the early years of developing Plasma Technology the founders had to undertake all the management functions of the company themselves. David Carr concentrated on marketing, sales and general management. John Ball used his technical experience to control production and product development. The founders' complementary skills in marketing and product innovation provided a sound management base from which to develop the company.

As the company has developed it has recruited additional managers to undertake specific tasks. There is now a core management team of five directors. The company has recruited an accountant, a manufacturing director and a sales director. This has allowed David and John to concentrate on their own specialist areas as marketing and technical directors respectively. The founders have tried not to adopt an autocratic style of management. The traditional management approach with 'a strong man at the top' is not their style. Decisions do have to be made but these are usually taken after a full open forum discussion with all management staff. Both founders have never been possessive about ownership or control of their company. Indeed, they have managed to maintain and improve their interest in the company and their own job satisfaction by delegating management functions. As the company has developed they have actively taken on staff to undertake areas of management which they do not enjoy or they find mundane. This has enabled them to concentrate on controlling the overall strategy of the company and to specialize in the management activities they find most interesting. Both have had no qualms about delegating control of certain areas of the company's activities; in many ways they have found it a relief to do so.

David Carr believes that when the company first started trading their complementary skills in marketing and technical development were a sufficient basis from which to develop the company. However, as the company has grown and become more successful a greater variety of management skills has been required, such as accountancy and production management. He believes many companies struggle to develop because they do not recruit enough management staff at an early stage. One reason for this is that some entrepreneurs jealously guard all control of their company and cannot bring themselves to relinquish control of even the smallest part by delegating activities. Plasma Technology has always tried to recruit top-quality managers. They get the best people available and the founders have no hesitation in employing people who are more able than themselves in running particular areas of the business.

One problem for the company has always been the decision of exactly when to take on new management staff. There is always a temptation to leave the decision until too late and only recruit when the existing managers are working to their limits in their own area of expertise and at the same time collectively trying to fill in the management area where a new recruit is needed. Plasma Technology has always tried to recruit new managers as early as financially possible so that newly appointed personnel have some time to become familiar with the company before they have a 'full' workload. In this way the pressure on existing managers is also relieved before it reaches a level where it could interfere with their main management activity. An example of this is the company's current consideration to appoint a personnel manager because existing managers have realized that the company has expanded to a level when more and more of their time is being taken up with personnel matters.

Plasma Technology has always tried to develop along 'fair' and ethical lines. The company is loyal to its workforce. It operates a profit-sharing scheme and all employees have been given shares in the company. Staff loyalty is reflected by the low level of staff turnover. The majority of staff who have joined the company are still with it today. However, on a limited number of occasions people have been recruited who have not been able to perform their job adequately. Since small companies cannot afford to carry these unsuitable employees they have been asked to leave.

Marketing, sales and exporting

David Carr knew from his previous marketing experience that it was important for Plasma Technology not to make the same mistake as some high technology companies. They were careful not to become too narrowly involved in technology and product development. They tried to ensure that they committed enough time and resources to selling their product. David Carr has always been a firm believer in the concept of companies being 'customer' driven, providing customers with what they want and not with what inventors think the customer needs.

The business plan, developed before the company started trading, provided a full list of names and addresses of potential customers. Initial response was very good and the company soon knew they had a good product which did provide customers with what they required. The company has always placed great importance on marketing and sales, particularly emphasizing face-to-face contact with potential customers. David Carr believes this is essential for many high technology companies because the complex nature of their product often needs to be explained fully to potential customers. This cannot always be done with trade adverts or circulars.

To promote the company's strategy of 'face-to-face' contact with clients they have always regularly attended national and international exhibitions. Exhibiting can be costly for many small businesses. However, costs can be reduced if, like Plasma Technology did in its early years, companies hire trailers and sales staff drive to venues. This may not be the best way to travel, particularly to continental destinations, but it was the cheapest, most effective way for Plasma Technology to develop sales. In later years when the company had become established the more luxurious option of flying to exhibitions and employing haulers to transport equipment could be afforded. Even with cost-cutting measures, exhibiting is still expensive, but David Carr believes it was one of the essential foundation stones in the development of Plasma Technology. Although he describes the process as 'painful', it did have benefits. The early sales successes gained through exhibitions and the raised company profile gained soon brought rewards.

Attendance at international exhibitions was also an essential prerequisite to achieve the company's goal of maximizing sales in overseas markets. The founders knew that they had a specialized product for which there was likely to be a good level of demand from both the UK and abroad. They knew that if their company was to become successful they would have to penetrate international markets, particularly Japan, West Germany and the USA. They also knew that if they concentrated only on the UK market they might become successful, but if there was a sudden downturn problems could arise. In 1984 this is exactly what did happen. Government became more stringent in its defence spending and demanded greater value for money. There was a partial collapse across the whole of the UK market in the demand for many types of high technology equipment. This affected Plasma Technology, but the company was able to overcome this problem by increasing its export sales. In 1984 they exported 40 per cent of output. After the downturn in UK demand they increased exports and in 1985 exported more than 70 per cent overseas. David Carr believes it is a very good insurance policy for companies producing high technology goods to think on an international scale and develop as wide an overseas sales base as possible, so that a downturn in one national economy will not jeopardize the company's future – a simple issue of not putting all one's eggs in one basket.

Developing overseas sales is not easy, as the problems and costs of exhibitions have already illustrated. One alternative that Plasma Technology tried was using overseas agents. They obtained very poor results, mainly because agents did not have either the ability or motivation to become technically involved in describing and selling their products. As a result of this and the downturn in the UK market, the company decided to set up small overseas subsidiaries operated by personnel from within the company. The first of these was set up in 1985 in the United States by a senior director of the company. He is now enjoying life abroad so much that he has decided to stay in the United States. Setting up this first subsidiary was, by the founder's own admission, a bit of a risk, but it was an immediate success. The subsidiary has continued to grow and a second subsidiary was opened in West Germany in 1986.

Plasma Technology, like many successful companies, place a great deal of reliance on their sales team. They always recruit good-quality, highly motivated salespeople and pay them well. In return they expect a lot. They are the only link in the company's philosophy of emphasizing direct sales and face-to-face contact with customers. The company adopts a very competitive attitude in marketing and sales and has regular meetings with salespeople to identify successes and, when appropriate, to discover why contracts have been lost.

Aspirations and company growth

When Plasma Technology started the founders had only modest aspirations for themselves and the business. They primarily started the company to become independent. They wanted the company to become profitable, but saw their business in terms of providing an enjoyable job and a reasonable income. Financial gain was not an aspiration when the company started.

The launch of Plasma Technology coincided with a new wave of research in microchips. New work was being developed to investigate the use of alternative materials to silicon and new microchip designs were also being tested. Growth in these activities was not predicted by the company's business plan. This lucky break, as David Carr describes it, greatly accelerated demand for their product. Plasma Technology carefully recorded what their customers required and developed plasma etching equipment to provide customers with the machines they needed. This increased demand in both the United Kingdom and abroad was one reason for the very rapid growth of the company.

It was only when the company was in its fourth year of growth and success that the founders realized they had developed the company into a very valuable business. Previously they had been too busy running the business to realize its success and value. It was at this point that the founders started to think about flotation on the Unlisted Securities Market (USM). They began to realize the full value of the company and slowly started to believe it would be prudent for them, their shareholding employees and the company to capitalize on their hard work and success. Flotation on the USM would provide security for the founders and their families and it would also provide the company with a cash injection to fund the future development of the business.

During 1984 and 1985 when they were considering flotation the company was in a healthy position (it had a price–earnings ratio of 15:1) and the high technology and electronics sectors of the USM and the Stock Exchange were very healthy. The founders decided to maintain control of the company and launch the remainder of the shares onto the USM in the autumn of 1986. The company was committed to this launch and when the Stock Market became a little jittery due to the 'big bang' they became a little worried about the launch. Preparations for the launch also coincided with a downturn in the semiconductor market. Their position did not therefore appear to be quite as bright as it had been when they first decided on the Unlisted Securities Market launch in 1985.

At this point the founders received two offers to take over the company. After negotiations they decided to accept a bid from Oxford Instruments, which took over the company in the summer of 1986. David Carr believes this move was the right one for the company, as well as for the founders, because the semiconductor industry was moving into a period of stability and maturity. He believed the industry would become dominated by fewer larger companies. By joining Oxford Instruments the company had access to this type of large company organization and to capital for expansion.

Despite becoming exceedingly wealthy as a result of the takeover both founders decided to stay with the company. They have continued to run Plasma Technology in almost exactly the same way as it was prior to the takeover and it has continued to expand.

Company strengths and weaknesses

When asked to look back over the development of Plasma Technology David Carr found it difficult to identify individual factors which had made the company successful. He thought luck played a large part in the early development of the company. The company's launch coincided with the new wave of research in the development of microchip technology. The company's ability to build on this lucky break by having a good product and aggressive marketing was also considered to be important. When the company started he was surprised at how supportive both customers and suppliers were for the new small business. But the founders have discovered that as the company has developed and become more successful the attitudes of most of its suppliers and customers have hardened.

The only regrets both founders have is the years they missed with their wives and children while developing the company. When asked if the company had made any mistakes David Carr suggested that they might have been a little too enthusiastic in publicizing the company's growth and development. He always thought that all publicity was good publicity and regularly distributed press releases. He believes this was very useful in the early development of the company but in recent years it might have attracted more companies to their very profitable market niche.

David Carr's five tips for success

(1) Research the market and business thoroughly prior to starting, then develop a good business plan.
(2) Operate in a market which you know and understand.
(3) Let the customer and marketing lead the business.
(4) Do not become a slave to one bank; consider changing when problems arise. Place little faith in professional advisers.
(5) Maintain staff loyalty and commitment; consider their views and conditions.

10
A Successful Company Providing Job Satisfaction and Independence:

John Brookfield

John Brookfield operates his electronics business from the Old Smithy in Culgaith, a small village some 10 km from Penrith in Cumbria. The company currently has a turnover of approximately £100,000 per year making a range of electrical and electronic components ranging from specialized transformers and switchgear to UVA fly catchers for the food industry. The business employs seven people, including his wife and daughter. John sees himself as a successful businessman. He has escaped the rat race of a large company and London to find the satisfaction of running his own business in the beautiful countryside of Cumbria.

Background

John Brookfield, a native of London, was educated at Faraday House Engineering College, where he undertook a course in electrical engineering. While at college he also learned the essence of improvisation in electrical engineering. Having become a chartered engineer John gained early experience with companies such as Landis and Gyr, makers of meters, and became fascinated by manufacturing processes and the use of electrical equipment. Subsequently power presses and winding gear enraptured John's imagination and sowed the seeds of his innovative desire to make electrical machinery.

In 1965 he joined the Post Office and spent 17 years working on a variety of projects as an electrical engineer. One major achievement included the development of a computer-controlled traffic recorder. John observes with delight how much of the expertise that went into the development of the product 22 years ago is still used in the same equipment today. He became dissatisfied with this particular development, largely because few superiors in higher management would accept the value of the use of computer control.

The Post Office then offered John the choice of working on two different projects: exchange design or power supply development. Both involved working as part of a large team. He became disillusioned by the lack of interest in his computer control system. With the aspiration of working for himself at the back of his mind John chose the power supply project. This work brought him into contact with lots of small businesses, many of whom were manufacturers, and gave him valuable insights into small business development and management.

At this time John's children were growing up, his father died and life in Wembley became more difficult for the family, especially his mother. Wembley began to experience increasing social problems common to the inner city, muggings and theft for example. These left the family increasingly concerned about safety. His children were both at private schools and financing their education was becoming increasingly problematical. The thought of sending the children to state schools in the area did not appeal so John began to think more and more about his future. The two issues of self-employment and moving away from Wembley were very closely interrelated. Initially John looked for suitable premises in Wembley but the high costs and rates, together with the difficulty of recruiting suitable staff, caused him to consider moving from London.

Although Londoners by birth, the Brookfields had connections with Cumbria. John's great grandfather had a farm at Newby, 16 km from Culgaith. This was sold some years ago but the family kept an acre or so of land with a barn near a river. The Brookfields hoped that one day they would convert this into a reasonable home. The family went to Cumbria regularly on holiday and each year spent four or five weeks in a caravan there. Consequently the family felt that they knew the area and the local people and were confident that if they moved up to Cumbria they would be accepted. This familiarity is important to John. Many people who try to opt out of the 'rat race' make haphazard decisions on their new location. Frequently, such moves do not work out because the people are not accepted. This, he suggests, is particularly the case in a village such as Culgaith, with its tightly knit community structure.

At the time he left British Telecom John Brookfield was an executive engineer earning £16,000 (in 1982). Somewhat discontent with the job and lack of prospects for his inventive mind, rather than money, were the factors which 'pushed' him into business. Since he has left, the unit in which he worked has been greatly reduced. John's fears of being made redundant at 45 with problems of re-employment, coupled with commitments of mortgages and school fees, were probably very accurate. While starting one's own business is far from secure, he took the view that jobs in all large firms can be equally insecure.

Developing the business

The process of developing the business began while he was still working for British Telecom. The idea was to sell his mother's home in Wembley and purchase a property in Cumbria where he could start in business. He regrets that the house he sold in Wembley did not realize as much as it should and he blames this on the image of Wembley in the London Borough of Brent. In the end they sold the London home for £45,000 and bought the Old Smithy in Culgaith for £35,000. The move was not as smooth as it might have been. The house sale in London was very protracted and this led to the Brookfields owning two houses for a period. Consequently, rather than starting afresh in Culgaith he commuted to Wembley for about a year. During this period he began to develop his idea and renovate the Old Smithy. The process of development was not, however, systematic. John did not produce detailed business plans and cash-flow forecasts. He 'knew' there was a market for his products, and this was adequate to satisfy his production capability and aspirations.

The smithy, which extends to some 230 m² , was in a semi-derelict condition. The roof, structural timbers and floors were in a bad state and needed considerable attention. The first major problem was to concrete the floors to give an appropriate load-bearing capacity for the machinery which he was going to require.

Early company development

Always an opportunist, John had bought a good deal of equipment and machinery from Plessey when they closed down their Liverpool factory. This purchase allowed him to equip a sheet metal shop with equipment worth over £100,000 for approximately £2,000. This opportunism has been typical of the way John has developed the business, which is equipped with machinery bought mostly at scrap value from the major electrical and electronics companies. This approach can of course create its own problems. The initial purchase had to be stored in a neighbouring barn for almost a year while floors were improved. Even now, a diesel generator stands out in the yard, covered in sheeting, until John finds space and time to install it.

John did have some help in the purchase and development of his workshop. His own attitude towards assistance is rather ambivalent. He is very independent and is reluctant to be told what to do. One of the great strengths of the company is John's confidence in his own ability to overcome and solve problems independently. He is also a firm believer in development out of cash flow; the amount of effort required to gain assistance, he thinks, is better put into the business itself. In the end he did gain an interest-free loan from Cumbria County Council. He would have preferred a grant!

John is sceptical about financial assistance and suggests that a business should stand up without subsidy. He is, though, very supportive of agencies such as COSIRA (the Council for Small Industries in Rural Areas) and of their advice and path clearing role. COSIRA was particularly important in helping to gain planning permission to use the smithy for his business. This was an issue about which many people objected. A closed village community has difficulty in accepting change and was afraid of the 'industrial' use to which the smithy was to be put. It is highly probable that the level of noise and nuisance from the workshop are less now than when the building was used as a smithy.

The process of restoration was slow and indeed is still continuing. It is the type of development project that may never be finished. This 'never finished' approach is typical of the way John is developing the business as a whole. The electronics 'boffin' in him constantly sees ways of improving and enhancing his products, in response not so much to market needs as to engineering excellence.

The smithy currently has five discrete workrooms. A small office and sheet metal shop are on the ground floor. Above this on the first floor are two rooms used for electrical and electronic assembly and transformer winding. To the rear of the building is a paint shop complete with metal cleaning plant and spray booth. The metal cleaning plant again was acquired courtesy of a large company closing down. The spray booth, designed and made by John, allows his employees to undertake spray work to the complete satisfaction of the factory inspectorate. In addition to the workshop, the Brookfields occupy the house attached to the smithy. The relationship of work and home is being re-enacted exactly as it might have been 200 years ago. The layout and feel of the entire workspace epitomizes the inventive enthusiast which is John Brookfield.

Product development

When he moved to Culgaith, John had some idea of what to produce, but it was not highly specified. Electrical goods, electrical components and telephone switchgear were the types of product he knew he could produce and sell. He had been involved with the development of such products while at British Telecom. He reasoned that he could produce them cheaper than other suppliers and hence would have a ready market. None of this was based on detailed market research. Much was based on intuition.

His product range is now based on a diversity of batch-produced equipment which the large companies cannot produce in small numbers. Margins are high. His basic product development philosophy is one of satisfying his own innovative mind, keeping his workforce employed and making a reasonable living.

Developing new market areas is a bit of a hit and miss affair, based on the considerable intuitive knowledge which John possesses. The lighting business developed from the UVA fly catchers he had been making. Electric fires are currently being made for a firm which got to know of him again by chance. John has a view of what he wants to do and what should generate income rather than adopting a systematic marketing strategy. The company does not advertise and does not see the need for advertising in the near future. His customers get to know about him by word of mouth. They return to do business with John because his products are well engineered, competitively priced and reliably delivered.

The company now employs five full-time and two part-time workers. This figure has varied over the past couple of years and was as high as seven full-time in 1986. The approach to employment is very flexible. The recent reduction in employees is the result of one person leaving to have a baby and the other moving away from the area. Such expansion and contraction are advantages of the Cumbrian environment. People are happy to do part-time work when they need it. John also has outworkers doing work at home. He suggests that this approach to employing people works well for his business and also for the local community. People now come to ask him for work. Wages are clearly lower than they are in London, although the company does pay quite well, especially compared with others in small rural villages in the local area. Despite initial suspicion, the village now sees his as an important role in the development of village life. He is able to expand and contract with his ideas and levels of demand without the onerous repercussions of laying people off and paying redundancy money.

Trading patterns and the aspirations of the workforce

To the outside observer, the remoteness of the Brookfield factory in Culgaith would be seen as a major problem for company trading, development or growth. The difficulties created, if indeed there are any, are compensated by other factors associated with living in such a pleasant environment. John Brookfield acknowledges that at times it can be difficult, but argues that distance is far less relevant than time. How long does it take to drive from Wembley to Croydon, he asks. Most of the products made by his company are small and easily fit into the back of his car. He is sure that many of his customers are impressed when he or his wife appears with the delivery of urgent goods. Few companies can offer such personal service. Most of his major customers are in the South of England and are serviced quite easily from Culgaith. The rest of his customers, mostly small in size, are scattered throughout the country. Supply to these customers can be difficult at times, but John Brookfield is philosophical about the problem. He is willing to continue trading with these small clients. They may get big one day and become a major customer. He maintains the stance that the customer is always right and tries to treat them accordingly. It is one of the problems of being a small business.

Future goals are diverse: John has toyed with making a business plan but does not really think business plans are particularly useful. After all, he argues, how can one know what the trading position will be in five years' time? He would like to be turning over £1m by year ten. At present, in the fourth year of business, turnover is approximately £110,000.

John's concern is with commitment to his workforce and employment in the village rather than achieving financial goals. He has never made anyone redundant and is anxious never to do so. However, he does have projects and products which could take him to the £1m turnover mark if all went well. He believes, for example, that there is scope to improve some of their existing products by introducing higher technology machinery and components. To do so would cost money and probably involve loans and grants. It may also alter his production methods and ultimately his way of life. It would certainly involve training staff and taking on more qualified people. This would modify his approach to the company and its management and remove the essence of its current success.

Brookfield Electronics have also identified new markets for existing products and new products. John discusses them with great enthusiasm. New products include power supply and standby lighting systems and telephone equipment. He believes the world is his oyster. He sees no major problems in making and marketing these products. He is both an optimist and a believer in his ability to produce engineering solutions to problems. This is the centre of his marketing strategy! This enthusiasm for problem-solving creates a very down-to-earth approach to business, but also one engulfed in humanism. He chooses what to do rather than being dictated to by the market. Brookfield Electronics believe it is not worth taking on work which they cannot cope with or trading with firms which do not pay. New markets are identified in a haphazard way, usually in discussion with current customers. The company does not have a formal marketing strategy. 'SWOTS' analysis (strengths, weaknesses, opportunities and threats) is irrelevant for the Brookfield organization. They have never made people redundant. Their production and sales policy, is designed with that in mind. Several longer-term orders are taken to maintain regular work for the workforce rather than to ensure profitability.

Competitive position is a key element in success, however. Most of the company's products are produced in small batches, frequently repeated, rather than larger production runs. In this context John Brookfield argues that lower technology production solutions are frequently very cost effective. The investment involved in digitally controlled machinery and tools for batch jobs is not worth while unless prices are high. With lower technology Brookfield Electronics can undercut competitors who have high technology equipment and higher overhead costs, and make useful profits. John Brookfield's engineering experience means that the company can frequently adapt this lower technology approach very profitably.

As the business grows Brookfield Electronics are being forced to consider new methods and approaches. A computer would be useful for wages, filing and invoicing for example. But at present the business can operate very well without one. Materials and stock control are issues to which they are giving attention, however. As production, and hence materials required, expand John has become increasingly aware of wastage in materials. When they were very small, wastage was not significant, but now it is something which they take very seriously. Mrs Brookfield is now involved in this side of the business. Quality control is also an issue receiving attention. It is difficult in a small business to dictate to employees about quality. John does not see himself as the 'management'; he believes the 'them and us' structure is quite inappropriate to his style of business. Hence he does not want to be seen to be 'checking up' on quality. His solution is to have a quality assurance scheme imposed on the company from outside. In this way it is not he who is imposing it and the family atmosphere of the business is not endangered.

Achievements

Brookfield Electronics is certainly a successful business. John regards himself as a lucky man, with a supportive family doing the thing he enjoys most. He lives in a part of the country which he likes away from the rat race. Interestingly, though, he does not get involved in the rural pursuits side of living in Cumbria. He has financial security and, most important to him, he has control over his life and lifestyle.

John Brookfield's five tips for success

When asked to select five secrets of success John Brookfield has difficulty in identifying just five. To him, success was a unique combination of factors all of which interact and interrelate differently at different times.

(1) The entrepreneur is an important factor in the development of any business. He or she needs determination, logic, enthusiasm, motivation, commitment and experience.
(2) The business idea or market should interest the entrepreneur and provide a challenge. Boredom is a sure road to failure.
(3) Hard work.
(4) A well-developed but flexible approach to planning. Constantly listening, thinking and responding to the market.
(5) Consider the workforce at all times. They are the mainstay of the business.

11
A Successful Co-operative:
Suma Wholefoods

Suma Wholefoods are located at Dean Clough Mill in Halifax. The co-operative's principle activity is the wholesaling of wholefoods. A small manufacturing plant also operates producing peanut butter and oils. There are plans to diversify into other products such as pills and potions. Current turnover is approximately £5 million. The co-operative has 28 full members and employs 10 additional workers on a casual part-time basis. Suma has been remarkably successful and has developed at a staggering pace to become one of the largest co-operatives in Great Britain. At present it is at a transition point in its development. Having recently moved to its new premises new opportunities are opening up. However, the market for wholefoods is becoming increasingly competitive. The co-operative is facing important decisions on its future development.

Background

The co-operative began trading in 1978 as a delivery service to members of the Federation of Northern Wholefood Collectives (FNWC). Suma became the only regional warehouse for the FNWC, although several were originally proposed. As a result Suma developed on the back of a captive market. FNWC was persuaded to buy from Suma because of the co-operative link although prices were frequently above those they could obtain elsewhere. The co-operative is registered as a Friendly Society and has adopted the rule structure of the Industrial Common Ownership Movement of which it is a member. As a consequence the assets are in common ownership and each member has one share in the company. If a member leaves the co-operative this share is given up because it is regarded more as a membership ticket than a share in the normal sense.

Like most co-operatives Suma has a strong philosophical base and it brings together people of like mind. Its philosophy relates first to working practice:

(1) Work must be fulfilling.
(2) There should be no hierarchical management structure with directors and workers; control must remain in the hands of the workers.
(3) The business operates for the benefit of workers as well as customers. Workers hire capital and not vice versa.
(4) Profits (or rather surpluses) not required by the business should be used for the development of other co-operatives or charitable ventures.

Growth of the business has been spectacular since its modest beginnings. Growth in turnover has averaged over 30 per cent in real terms. In the early years of the co-operative, growth reached well over 50 per cent per year in real terms. This was possible because of the particular market niche which the company occupied. Very little of the growth was due to a conscious effort to develop the market or the use of market research or aggressive marketing policies. Indeed, such procedures and policies ran counter to the philosophy of the co-operative. Growth was based on the growing numbers of independent wholefood retailers. Schools, hospitals and other public-sector organizations also increased their demand for Suma's products. However, the development of the public-sector links has been difficult because of tight price constraints which many of these organizations have been forced to adopt. Development of the market has been largely by mailing price lists to customers and potential customers who then respond with orders either by post or phone. More recently Suma has developed a more positive approach to marketing and does undertake some advertising. Their marketing representatives make regular visits to all customers.

The market base of the co-operative has changed slightly over its history. The FNWC link has slowly declined as Suma has taken over its function as a leading northern wholefood collective with Suma providing a buying, packaging, branding and distribution function for the members. The *raison d'être* for FNWC has disappeared. The market area of Suma has also expanded to cover the North of England and areas as far south as Leicestershire. The geographical extent of the market has been agreed with other wholefood wholesalers, both co-operative and non-co-operative, with whom Suma has good operating relations. Rather than being in direct competition a group of wholesalers operate co-operatively even to the extent of intertrading. This loose confederation of the wholesalers may be further formalized in future as market conditions and competition become more difficult.

Early company development

Suma was originally located in the Calls in Leeds, a rundown area which had for a long time been identified for redevelopment. Originally they rented the ground floor of a large building. As business expanded they occupied the first and second floors. Finally they moved into the third floor as well, and eventually they bought the building. Neither the building nor the area was ideal for a growing company. Road access was very difficult along narrow streets, making access for lorries extremely difficult. Customer access was also difficult as Suma had to rely on on-street parking for customers. The 3,350 m² building was badly laid out for efficient operation. Goods were stored on the third floor and had to be moved down for packing and distribution. Over a two- or three-year period it became increasingly clear that their premises were a problem and that alternatives had to be found.

Dean Clough was decided on after a search of the local area during 1986. The co-operative looked at property in Leeds, Wakefield and Bradford as well as Halifax. Although property in Leeds might have been ideal locationally, the co-operative felt that it could not sustain either the high rentals or prices quoted for freehold property. As with many location decisions the co-operative chanced on Dean Clough at a late stage in negotiations for a property in Bradford.

The unit at Dean Clough, the former Crossley Carpet complex in Halifax, is ideal for their needs. The close-knit working community and supportive working philosophy engendered by Ernest Hall, the owner of Dean Clough, is very appropriate for the co-operative. It now has 6,870 m² of good-quality space, most of which is at ground-floor level. This should be more than adequate for the development of the co-operative in the foreseeable future, unless it decides to diversify more heavily into manufacturing.

Rentals are typical of those offered at Dean Clough. The first year is rent free, allowing the co-operative to settle in, building up to an eventual figure of £130,000 p.a. after three years. This rental, while low by regional as well as national standards, is one of the stimuli to development and change within the co-operative. Members are fully aware that turnover will have to be increased to cover this additional burden in the longer term.

Suma completed its relocation with very few problems. As with all the decisions of the co-operative all members were involved in the decision. This was a long drawn-out process taking months rather than weeks. All were in favour of the move. Most of the members at that time lived in the Leeds area with one or two in Huddersfield and Halifax so that an incentive was offered to overcome the problems of movement. Some members have left the co-operative since the move to take up other opportunities, particularly in higher education.

Suma have now become fully established at Dean Clough. Relocation has not led to the loss of business although some adjustments have been made. Halifax is some distance from the main centres in West Yorkshire and is less accessible to the motorway network. Suma have noticed that fewer customers call in to collect orders and more rely on the Suma delivery system. Overall delivery provision and transport costs do not seem to have been adversely affected by relocation. The more efficient site access and loading facilities more than compensate for any problems. The move has permitted Suma to develop a full cash and carry service which they were unable to offer in Leeds. This takes advantage of the good lay-out of the single-storey warehouse. Although the cash and carry service may have been more successfully located in Leeds, Suma are pleased with developments in the first year of operation. Whether because of the move, the new style of operation or simply natural progress in development of the co-operative, administration duties appear to have increased since relocating.

The co-operative philosophy and management

Suma were established as a collectively run business and still operate in this way, although some minor modifications have been made. It is likely that major changes will be seen in the near future. The formal decision-making body is the general meeting and until recently all decisions were taken by that body. The general meeting is held weekly on Wednesday afternoon when business is over. Because some people are absent from the meeting, drivers out delivering for example, decisions of the meeting are ratified at the next meeting. When the co-operative was smaller decisions were taken by consensus. But as membership grew this became an unwieldy approach to decision-making and a 75 per cent majority rule was adopted in 1983.

The structure of decision-making, a common problem in all co-operatives, was particularly problematic for Suma. A considerable amount of time was taken up by meetings which were frequently ill prepared. Long discussions took place over relatively minor matters while major issues received less than full consideration. Many of the new members simply did not have the necessary information to take an active part in decision-making. Although in theory the principle of co-operative management was operated, in practice not all members were able to participate. A new structure was introduced in 1985 as a result of a decision at a general meeting. Two new committees were set up, one dealing with finance and the other with personnel. Both committees were established to solve existing problems. In the case of the finance committee, the co-operative realized that over time they had simply started to respond to conditions as they occurred rather than establish goals and objectives. In the fields of marketing, buying and finance there was little if any co-ordination and no attention was paid to performance, targeting and monitoring. The personnel committee was established to solve the many problems which arose from the rotation of staff between different tasks in different parts of the business. As part of its operating philosophy the co-operative encouraged the rotation of staff. When the co-operative was small and tasks relatively simple this was fine and permitted the goals of job satisfaction and efficient manning to be achieved. As long as everyone had a working knowledge of each aspect of the business, illness or crisis could be overcome efficiently by the group rallying around. However, as the co-operative grew, tasks became more specialized, requiring longer training periods and longer rotation periods. It soon became evident that the satisfaction gained from rotation was frequently at the expense of performance and efficiency.

While overall policy decisions are still the responsibility of the general meeting, the finance committee provides a strategic framework for the development of the business as well as making decisions on purchases of routine and non-routine items. The personnel committee provides an overview on issues such as recruitment, disputes, pay and conditions and labour planning. Membership of these committees comes from each of the seven areas of the business. While these two committees have brought some structure to the rather chaotic management of a rapidly expanding business, problems still remain with the general meeting and, as will be seen later, organizational change is still in progress. Other less formal meetings are held to discuss specific issues and make recommendations to the general meeting.

The workforce

Many of the changes in Suma are associated with changing membership patterns and particularly the declining dominance of men within the organization. While men previously dominated the workforce, women now make up nearly half of the total workforce. The recruitment of staff is a long process. Some workers are recruited simply on the basis of the task to be undertaken and are employees of the co-operative. If the co-operative needs an HGV driver, for example, it will simply recruit one on the open market. Normally, however, candidates apply to become members of the co-operative. New workers are given a week's trial before being accepted for the job. It can take up to a year for new workers to be nominated and accepted for membership of the co-operative. Generally the co-operative looks for particular personal attributes which will help the individual to fit successfully into the organization rather than specific work skills. In this way the co-operative tends to attract particular types of people sympathetic to the co-operative ethos. Many are educated to degree level and beyond.

Pay is an important element of work at Suma and one in which the co-operative philosophy is maintained. Everyone, including casual and temporary workers, is paid an equal wage net of tax. Additional payments of £500 p.a. are made to those supporting children. Bonuses are paid according to the performance of the business. The working day can be very long at Suma. Although there is some flexibility in working hours, many work a very long day to the point of self-exploitation. Conditions of employment are, however, good with generous sick leave, maternity/paternity leave and a non-contibutory pension. Although members do voice dissatisfaction about Suma this is concerned with the decision-making structure and self-exploitation rather than with more fundamental issues. The self-exploitation issue is likely to continue because of the very nature of the co-operative organization.

Growth and reorganization

Moving to Halifax in 1986 was a major change and stimulus for development within the co-operative. It is still adapting to many of these changes. Relocation was not the only stimulus for development. Suma are faced with increasing market competition and organizational problems associated with their growing success.

Size has increasingly been a problem for Suma which no longer class themselves as a small organization. The decision-making process which has operated within Suma since their foundation, with the weekly general meeting as the focus for major decisions, has become too cumbersome for the efficient operation of the co-operative. But to maintain the co-operative structure it is vital that a non-hierarchical decision-making structure is maintained, which provides decision-making involvement for all members. New proposals are currently being discussed which will introduce a more decentralized structure operating as a series of functional sectors, each operating and contributing to the co-operative's trading procedures. Agreed in principle by 24 of the 29 full members of the co-operative the new system should be in operation in 1988. In essence the co-operative wants to keep the strengths of small group working, in which everyone has the knowledge and capability to substitute for others without the associated inefficiencies of this approach which occur in larger organizations. In the past couple of years the general meeting has become unsatisfactory, first because of the difficulty in controlling a general meeting of 25–30 people and second because of the gross inefficiency of halting production while the meetings take place.

Suma set up a group to look at other ways of organizing the co-operative which would remedy these problems. Unlike most other larger co-operatives and businesses, which turn to the line management principle, Suma adopted a system of autonomous segments each responsible for the fundamental element of the business whether it be buying, warehousing or manufacturing. This would allow each segment to be made up of about seven members. Each segment would be responsible for the efficient operation of that segment. Each segment would send a member to a group linking together all the segments which would be responsible for the efficient co-ordination of segments for the benefit of Suma as a whole. A dialogue would then take place between the co-ordinating group and the segments so that decisions could be taken without involving the whole co-operative simultaneously, and hence bringing the organization to a halt, but still allowing all members a say in decision-making. It is currently undecided whether the co-ordinating group will have authority to make major decisions or whether a full general meeting will still be required. The designation of segments will not prevent the movement of members between tasks in different segments as the ability to move around and the knowledge and ability so gained are still seen as crucial elements of the success of the co-operative.

Marketing and future developments

Incredibly Suma have given very little attention to market research and market-ing in its development. Success has been almost by accident on the crest of a developing market. Market conditions are changing. Suma are beginning to see a halt in market expansion. These changes are brought about by two major causes. First, the supermarket chains are beginning to compete in the wholefoods market and they are offering a range of the more straightforward products which might be seen as Suma's 'bread and butter'. Because of their buying power many of these products can be retailed below Suma prices. Second, other wholefood wholesalers are entering the market and disturbing the equilibrium which has existed for some time. Some of the newer additions to the market are able to offer products below Suma prices by what appear to be loss-making pricing policies and are in addition offering services, such as next-day delivery, which Suma at present cannot offer. To adapt to each of these forms of competition puts Suma in a dilemma. It would be possible for the co-operative to supply the supermarkets with some of their products and as a consequence share in some of the supermarket success. This would, however, be contrary to the underlying philosophy of Suma which was built up from the growth and loyalty of the small retailers. To grow with the supermarkets may well put the small retailer out of business. To compete with the new wave of wholesalers would necessitate forsaking many of the current working practices. Rather than imposing further on members in order to maintain market share, many members wish to see working conditions and hours improved.

The co-operative also needs to research fairly basic market issues such as packaging sizes and product demand. Little attempt has been made in the past to respond to even these basic aspects of the market-place. Some change has and is taking place in this direction, to retain the position of the small shops which Suma supply. The maintenance of these outlets is vital both practically and philosophically. Recently products have been offered to these outlets pre-packaged in own label packs. These packs look more attractive than the traditional brown bags and provide a comparable image to the supermarket packaging. Suma have also been looking to expand their markets in two other directions. First, they have been focusing their attention on the catering side of the wholefood business. In particular they have targeted university catering as a possible growth area where concentrations of health-minded customers are currently not having their dietary needs fulfilled. In addition the co-operative is beginning to export its products. Exporting is still in its infancy representing probably as little as 2 per cent of turnover. However, certain European countries have been identified and co-operative members are attending European trade missions and exhibitions.

Although the co-operative has reached a point in its development which requires it to give serious thought to the future, it has already adapted very rapidly to the problems associated with moving premises which, for most companies, can be a traumatic experience. The co-operative has the mechanisms to cope with, and adapt to, future opportunities and difficulties.

Achievements

Suma have so far been far more successful than most co-operatives, a fact which they attribute to a clutch of key factors.

The co-operative structure of Suma and the individuals within the co-operative have been very much part of its success. The operation of the co-operative has involved very long working hours on the part of all members. They have all had the same aims for the co-operative and all have given their time in an unselfish manner, making their own interests secondary to those of the co-operative. The approach to working practices in which individual members have control over their own work, the chance to move to new jobs and acquire new skills and the lack of a rigid management structure all contribute to a successful business.

In the mid-1970s the wholefood philosophy and market were expanding, but it was very much a minority market, mainly including the better educated, more affluent members of the middle classes. The message of better eating, better living is now part of national belief and has been capitalized by more politicians and marketing people. However, the precise choice of product line was almost incidental to Suma.

Suma provide an excellent service to their customers and are able to offer three-day delivery. The personal service offered by members who are deeply involved in the success of the co-operative is one of Suma's key selling points and one which makes a major contribution to their success.

Luck has played its part in the successful development of the co-operative. This has been most important in product development in which Suma have found themselves with the right product at the right time. Had the co-operative selected a different product, members are doubtful whether success would have been assured.

Suma's five tips for success

(1) A co-operative structure with a full commitment to this philosophy by all members.

(2) Hard work and the unselfish commitment of members to the development of the co-operative.
(3) The choice of a product in a growing market.
(4) Provide an excellent personal service for customers.
(5) Luck.

12
A Review of the Factors Contributing to Success

The focus for this book has been an investigation of the factors contributing to small business success. The introductory chapters identified a variety of definitions for success and the differing goals to which many businesses aspire. The existence of goals relating to finance, independence, creativity, job satisfaction and other objectives was confirmed by the business advisers who have contributed chapters to this book.

The case studies have exemplified how the different goals can be achieved and how an interrelationship between them can be sustained. All the case study companies showed a desire for independence when they started and this aspiration is still important. By maintaining their independence Suma Wholefoods have been able to adopt a co-operative working environment and achieve high levels of job satisfaction and other 'socially' orientated objectives. Independence has provided John Brookfield with an outlet for his creative ambitions. Achievement of these two goals has led to job satisfaction and a lifestyle with which John is very content. Tom Farmer of Kwik-Fit and David Carr and John Ball of Plasma Technology have developed financially successful companies. This has allowed all three to enhance their job satisfaction and maintain their independence. In the case of Plasma Technology the latter two goals were, to some extent, enhanced by the takeover of their company by Oxford Instruments. As their case study shows, this action, which is usually considered as imposing restrictions on a company, has had a beneficial impact on the company and its two founders. Indeed, it may enable them to develop new products and enhance their creative ambitions in the future.

Analysis of the case studies

The four case studies were selected to exemplify particular types of success:

(1) Financial success – Kwik-Fit.
(2) Creativity – Plasma Technology.
(3) Job satisfaction – John Brookfield Electronics.
(4) Independence – Suma Wholefoods Co-operative.

However, as the preceding brief review showed, the overlap between goals and aspirations is considerable. No one common view of success was adopted. Instead, for all four, their criteria for success related to a number of different factors. The mix between these factors only really became apparent as interviews developed and for the first time the businesses consciously evaluated what they received or wanted from the business.

Although none of the case study companies had ever adopted a fixed idea of success they all had a strongly single-minded idea of what they wanted to do. John Brookfield left British Telecom to break free of the constraints imposed by a large organization. He moved to the Lake District determined to fulfil his own creative potential and set up a business which would provide him with more job satisfaction than he had ever achieved at British Telecom. The Suma Wholefoods Co-operative was set up with very clear working practices and a strong common-ownership philosophy. Using this structure it has been able to develop a market for its wholefood products and has become one of the largest co-operatives in Great Britain. David Carr and John Ball of Plasma Technology left their previous jobs with a strong desire to start in business on their own. They knew they had a good idea for a new product at a competitive price and have single-mindedly developed the product and brought it to the market. Their ambition was to develop a good product and sell it successfully. The fact that this goal could provide financial rewards appears to have been secondary to their considerations during the development of the business.

All of the case studies highlight how goals and aspirations can change over time. The founders of Plasma Technology started their business determined to succeed in bringing their plasma etching equipment to the market. In the early years of the development of the business it was not unusual for them to tackle any task and work 24-hour days. Success in selling their product has enabled them to take on more staff. Increasingly their own job satisfaction has become important and both now specialize in the management activities they find most interesting. In contrast, Tom Farmer of Kwik-Fit started in business determined to become financially successful. He was a millionaire at the age of 30 and financially secure. As a result his criteria for success have changed. Financial success of the company is still paramount in his considerations but he now gains considerable personal rewards from his ability as a motivator and enthusiast showing off his company. Personal job satisfaction in this work is now important to him.

The case studies show that changes in company operating structure often arise as a result of growth in employment and turnover. However, growth in more traditional measures of company success, such as turnover and profit, sometimes goes unnoticed. The Suma Wholefoods Co-operative was developed with a structure which placed a strong emphasis on job satisfaction. The fact that after only 12 years' trading they had developed a company with a turnover of £5 million was not considered to be overly important by the members. For them other goals are far more important. This situation might have been predicted for a co-operative organization but a similar realization occurred at Plasma Technology. The founders were almost unaware of their own financial success. Turnover and profit were important 'by-products' of the successful development of their plasma etching equipment. It was not until the fourth year of the company's development that, almost by accident, they realized they had developed not only a successful product but also a very valuable business with a turnover of approximately £3 million. It was also only after this time period that they had sufficient confidence to realize that their success could continue and it was not just 'a flash in the pan'.

Success, under whatever criteria, does not seem to have dramatically changed the founders' views of their priorities and aspirations for themselves or their companies. Despite financial success the Suma Wholefoods Co-operative has rigidly maintained its common-ownership principles. David Carr and John Ball of Plasma Technology have remained relatively unaffected by their company's growth and the financial rewards it has brought them. They have always tried to develop the company on fair and ethical lines. Staff conditions and loyalty have always been important to them and they have been able to share some of the company's financial success by introducing a profit-sharing scheme for the workforce. John Brookfield's views and criteria for success appear to have become more deep-rooted as the business develops. Finding an outlet for his creative abilities and job satisfaction are still important; he tends to undertake jobs which he will enjoy in preference to undertaking work which may be more profitable. Some larger, less interesting jobs are accepted, but these are usually undertaken to ensure the continued security of his local workforce.

Despite their diverse goals the four case studies appear to have a number of similarities. The most important of these appears to be the fact that by accident or desire each company has developed new products or services. For all four this seems to have been an important element of the company's success. Even in his retirement from tyre sales in the United States Tom Farmer was looking at new market opportunities. He saw the potential for 'one-stop' exhaust centres and developed Kwik-Fit in the United Kingdom. David Carr and John Ball of Plasma Technology identified a gap in a market and carefully developed a product and undertook market research to ensure their hunch was correct. Wholefoods were not a new concept when Suma started trading in 1976 but there were few wholesalers concentrating solely on this market. The subsequent dramatic growth in the market, due to concern about food additives and colouring and an increase in environmental considerations, has enabled them to provide an almost unique service for public- and private-sector organizations and individuals throughout the North of England. One of John Brookfield's reasons for starting in business was to develop an outlet for his creative abilities. Therefore he is regularly developing new products.

Some commentators have argued that small companies should pursue a passive role when developing their business and rely on producing goods already accepted by consumers and develop a niche within an existing market. This view is generally adopted because it is thought that small businesses do not have the resources or expertise to market new products effectively. As the case studies have shown this view appears to be unfounded and new product development can be an important element of small business success.

Analysis of the entrepreneurs' tips for success

All the entrepreneurs in the case study companies gave five tips for success. These are presented at the end of each chapter (Chapters 8–11). Their different goals, size, products and services might have been expected to produce a diverse range of advice. However, it is interesting that their tips have a number of common features. More formal management considerations such as planning and marketing are noted, but these are often described in the context of the operations of the company. Other operational features such as people and hard work are also considered to be important contributions. These areas are reviewed separately. The entrepreneurs' tips can be seen in Table 12.1.

Planning

All the case study companies acknowledged the importance of good planning. David Carr of Plasma Technology noted that the planning process should begin before the company starts trading with thorough research of the market and the business. He believes that the development of a good business plan prior to starting was one of the key elements to Plasma Technology's success. This view is strongly supported by Tom Farmer of Kwik-Fit. The development of his company has been based on careful planning and forecasting. The company's investment in a computerized management information system aids the development of both planning and reviews of performance against previous plans. The importance of planning is now taken for granted at Kwik-Fit. Even John Brookfield, who has a slightly more relaxed view of the world of small business, notes the need for a well-developed but flexible approach to planning. The Suma Wholefoods Co-operative had a slightly different view of planning to the other

Table 12.1   The entrepreneurs' tips for success

Tom Farmer – Kwik-Fit
(1) Policies and mechanisms for motivating staff are vital to success.
(2) Commitment from all staff is vital. This is perhaps most important at senior management level.
(3) Knowing the market and changes in market demand is essential.
(4) Decisions to enter new markets or develop new products need to be based on careful forecasting and planning.
(5) Management control is important, particularly in retail organizations. Computerization for control systems and the provision of up-to-the-minute management information are beneficial.

David Carr – Plasma Technology
(1) Research the market and business thoroughly prior to starting, then develop a good business plan.
(2) Operate in a market which you know and understand.
(3) Let the customer and marketing lead the business.
(4) Do not become a slave to one bank; consider changing when problems arise. Place little faith in professional advisers.
(5) Maintain staff loyalty and commitment; consider their views and conditions.

John Brookfield – John Brookfield Electronics
(1) The entrepreneur is an important factor in the development of any business. He or she needs determination, logic, enthusiasm, motivation, commitment and experience.
(2) The business idea or market should interest the entrepreneur and provide a challenge. Boredom is a sure road to failure.
(3) Hard work.
(4) A well-developed but flexible approach to planning. Constantly listening, thinking and responding to the market.
(5) Consider the workforce at all times. They are the mainstay of the business.

Suma Wholefoods Co-operative
(1) A co-operative structure with a full commitment to this philosophy by all members.
(2) Hard work and the unselfish commitment of members to the development of the co-operative.
(3) The choice of a product in a growing market.
(4) Provide an excellent personal service for customers.
(5) Luck.

companies. They probably had the most rigidly applied plans of all the companies interviewed, but their plans primarily concern the co-operative's common-ownership philosophy rather than its activities in the market-place. For Suma the product was almost incidental, a co-operative structure was important and they believe their plans to develop in this way have been a large element in their success.

Marketing

Marketing was the second area of importance about which all the case study companies agreed. The market was viewed by the companies as the arena in which they had to operate; to perform well they all knew they had to provide the products and/or services required by the market. The companies knew their market well and had very practical views about what it required and how best to market their product or service.

The importance of knowing and understanding the market was considered to be very important by David Carr. He also noted that the customer and marketing should lead the business. Tom Farmer supported these views and suggested that the market needs to be carefully monitored so that companies can recognize developing opportunities and understand their capabilities, strengths and weaknesses. John Brookfield succinctly described the importance of marketing as the constant need to listen, think and respond to the market.

The importance of serving a market effectively was described by all the case studies. The two distribution-orientated companies also noted the importance of services in their tips for success. The slogan of the 'Kwik-Fit fitter' jingle is 100 per cent satisfaction, and one of the key elements of the company's success is thought to be their commitment to customer satisfaction. Suma also identified excellent personal service as a major contribution to their success.

The workforce

The final area in which there was unanimous agreement in the tips given by all four case studies concerns the importance of the workforce. All the companies noted that the quality and commitment of the workforce had a strong influence on success. John Brookfield described them as the mainstay of the business and suggested that they should be considered at all times. This view was supported by David Carr who also noted the need to maintain their loyalty and commitment. His company had developed a profit-sharing scheme. This was introduced as a method of rewarding a loyal workforce for the development of a financially successful company. Kwik-Fit have a similar scheme and Tom Farmer observed that methods of motivating staff are vital to success. The Suma Wholefoods Co-operative's whole philosophy revolves around equality and the importance of the workforce; it therefore comes as little surprise that two of their tips emphasize the importance of the workforce. The co-operative's ability to allow individual members to control their work, acquire new skills and change jobs was thought to contribute to the success of the business.

Hard work

Three out of the four case studies acknowledged the importance of hard work and commitment in the successful development of their companies. Tom Farmer noted that he and his family 'eat, drink and sleep Kwik-Fit' and he expects similar commitment from senior staff. The success of the Suma Wholefoods Co-operative has been based on the commitment of its members and their involvement in working very long hours. John Brookfield also noted hard work as one of his tips for success. The only company which did not specifically record hard work as a tip for success was Plasma Technology. Since the founders were regularly involved in working 24-hour days to meet deadlines during the early development of the company they could be expected to support the importance of this advice.

The remaining tips suggested by the case studies generally concerned particular snippets of advice or experience which the businesses had found beneficial. John Brookfield suggested that it is essential for the entrepreneur to remain interested in the product or market. He regards boredom or the lack of a challenge as a sure road for failure. During their development Plasma Technology had problems in obtaining finance from banks. David Carr suggested that a change of bank can help to resolve these problems.

The final tip offered by Suma is luck. They suggest that it played an important part in their success. They believe Suma found itself with the right product at the right time. Although David Carr did not specifically mention luck as a tip he noted that Plasma Technology had a similar lucky break. The launch of their plasma etching equipment coincided with a new wave of research in the development of microchip technology. It is frequently difficult to distinguish between luck and well-calculated planning. To some people, it is lucky if the plan works successfully, to others that is the purpose of planning. For Kwik-Fit, luck has played a role in the development of the company, but this development was well planned and carefully considered.

It is impossible to know what might have happened to these businesses or other companies without their lucky break. It is possible that through their business expertise they would have changed to serve markets which offered a better prospect of success (under whatever criteria they may use to define the term). Equally, it is possible they may not have been successful. The existence and importance of luck are acknowledged to differing degrees by commentators.

Analysis of the advisers' tips for success

At the end of their chapters (Chapters 4–7) all the business advisers who contributed to this book gave their five tips for success. It is interesting to compare the advice which they provide. As might have been expected Harry Nicholls from Aston Science Park has a tendency to concentrate on new high

Table 12.2 The contributors' tips for success

Paul Foley – Market survey

(1) Decide how you want the company to develop and what rewards you want to obtain from the business (financial, social and others).

(2) Prepare and review business plans on a regular basis. Use the reappraisal process as an opportunity to review goals and objectives and to identify strengths and weaknesses in the company.

(3) Know the market and identify what it is the customers want to buy. Use this information to develop marketing management policies to maintain or exploit the company's position within the market.

(4) Be aware of opportunities to develop new products which fill a gap in the market.

(5) Do not rely heavily on one customer and consider carefully all the consequences of accepting the 'big order'.

Alan Pickering – The financial view

(1) Plan and run your business with the benefit of all available expert operational and financial advice.

(2) Create the broadest possible financial base for the business and ensure your personal financial exposure is limited and tolerable.

(3) Always base your plans and budgets on a thorough study of existing or new markets. Every business should be market-led and not product-driven.

(4) Aim for steady, profitable growth and ensure you create and develop the management team needed to handle expansion.

(5) Make sure you create and use those operational and financial controls which will enable you to make prompt and well-informed choices among available options.

Harry Nicholls – The high technology view

(1) High technology entrepreneurs need to understand that technology is a means to an end. Developing new technology is very interesting but it will not usually 'pay for itself'.

(2) The product needs to serve a market, and this market usually has to have the potential for growth.

(3) The entrepreneur has to be willing to take risks, but these risks should be tempered by an appreciation of the business and the market-place.

(4) Companies need to develop and understand their business plan, but flexibility is required because the world is not always the same as they thought it was or will be. Companies need to learn from their experience and be able to take good advice.

(5) It has to be accepted that as the company grows, the company will have to change. Growth will often necessitate the requirements of new personnel and possibly the entrepreneur being placed on the sidelines.

Peter Lovell – The business adviser's view

(1) Know the break-even point for the business. This is the one indicator which can turn triumph to disaster, or vice versa.

(2) Do not confuse profit and cash (or vice versa). Cash does not necessarily mean profit, and profit does not necessarily mean cash. Most businesses would be wise to acknowledge this before they start to produce both profit forecasts (or budgets), as well as cash flow forecasts.

(3) Be wary of the 'big order'. Many firms come unstuck by accepting an order which is too large for their production capacity, for their finances, or for their management to handle.

(4) Be proud of the company. Lack of pride and confidence will soon communicate itself to staff and customers alike, and can only lead to eventual failure.

(5) Be lucky!

---

technology companies and their strategies, and Alan Pickering of Yorkshire Enterprises Ltd favours financial considerations. Paul Foley and Peter Lovell take a rather broader view of success and strategies. Despite their differing backgrounds and interests the contributors give tips and advice which are broadly similar.

Their tips primarily concentrate on three main areas: planning, marketing and risk minimization. Other factors, best described as operational factors, are also suggested by two of the contributors. These areas are reviewed separately. The advisers' tips are listed in Table 12.2.

Planning

There is a general agreement among most of the advisers that successful companies require a clearly developed business plan. Paul Foley suggests this plan should consider the entrepreneurs' personal goals and ambitions as well as the normal criteria included in the company's business plan. Alan Pickering recommends that the business plan and the business should be developed with the benefit of all available expert operational and financial advice. However, as Harry Nicholls points out, one problem for many entrepreneurs is taking advice, another difficulty is being able to distinguish good advice from bad.

There is general agreement that business plans must be supported by a regular review. This reappraisal provides the company with an opportunity to review goals and objectives and identify company strengths and weaknesses. In addition to this reappraisal, usually undertaken on a yearly basis, Peter Lovell suggests that at the very least the company should know its break-even point and constantly monitor its performance against this measure. Alan Pickering advocates that there should be sufficient operational and financial controls so that company performance can be examined more regularly than a simple yearly review of the business plan. Such operational controls enable the company to monitor performance effectively and make prompt, well-informed choices when required.

Marketing

The second main area of agreement between the advisers concerns the importance of marketing for company success. To maintain or increase sales companies need to provide the market with what it requires. To do this effectively and profitably companies need to know their market and identify what its customers require. Market research does not have to be highly sophisticated, but it is essential that some market research is undertaken before developing a company or entering a new market.

Continuous monitoring of the market should also be undertaken. A particular problem which can occur among companies developing new products was identified by Harry Nicholls. He warned entrepreneurs against developing new technology or products as an exercise in itself; they must serve a market and pay for themselves. This overall view was probably put most succinctly by Alan Pickering who noted that every business should be market-led not product-driven.

Risk minimization

The advisers noted the risks involved in developing a business and all four gave a tip to reduce the level of risk. Alan Pickering suggested financial risks and exposure could be limited by creating a broad financial base and reducing personal financial exposure to a tolerable level. Paul Foley advocated the minimization of trading risks by not relying too heavily on one customer and carefully considering the consequences of the big order. This latter point was also supported by Peter Lovell. Harry Nicholls' advice concerning risks was rather more general in nature, suggesting that entrepreneurs should have a willingness to take risks but that this should be tempered by an appreciation of the business and market-place.

The remaining tips suggested by the advisers were primarily concerned with factors affecting the operating structure of the business. The most important of these was suggested by Harry Nicholls who noted that as companies grow they need to develop their management structure, often necessitating the recruitment of new personnel and sometimes placing the entrepreneur on the sidelines. The need to develop a good management team to handle expansion was also noted by Alan Pickering. Peter Lovell was the only adviser to stray from hard factual guidelines when he suggested that luck was a requirement for success.

Comparison of the advisers' and entrepreneurs' tips for success

All the contributors noted that success can be interpreted in different ways by different businesses. Despite the diversity of goals which businesses can adopt, and the case studies exemplified this range, all the contributors gave a common set of strategies and tips for success. None specified particular tips or activities to achieve different success criteria. In general it seems that a common set of tips and strategies can assist the development of any company. It appears that a well-run company observing these tips could be a successful company whatever its criteria for success.

There are a number of similarities and differences between the entrepreneurs' and advisers' tips, strategies and views of success. The two groups present their advice from slightly different viewpoints. The entrepreneurs, having been personally involved in the successful development of their business, generally had a very practical view of the problems and opportunities involved in developing a business. Their tips and advice for success had a practical orientation based on the experience of developing their own business. The advisers have seen many thousands of businesses during their work. Although their breadth of experience was wider than that of the entrepreneurs it generally lacked the depth of practical knowledge which the latter had acquired. As a result the advisers tended to give more factually based tips and advice, often based on the broader generalities of developing a business.

The main similarities between the two groups concerned the importance of planning and marketing to company development. All the advisers and case studies noted the importance of these two areas. The two are complementary and form the basis of what is commonly accepted as a well-run business. An amalgamation of all the tips and advice given about these two areas suggests that planning should commence before the business starts trading. A business plan should be developed which clearly outlines goals, objectives and a clear development path for the business. These plans should be supported by suitable monitoring techniques and performance reviews undertaken on a regular basis to analyse strengths and weaknesses. The markets and marketing should lie at the heart of the business plan. One of the objectives which should form the basis for a plan is providing the market with what it requires. To maintain or improve the company's position in the market, market research and monitoring are important. These will identify opportunities and threats and allow the business to respond to changes in the market or take advantage of gaps in the market.

Whatever criteria for success a business has, it appears that good planning and marketing are essential. A well-run company developed with an emphasis in these two areas should have a clearer understanding of what it is trying to achieve and thus possess a good idea of how it is performing.

The main difference which the advisers noted and the entrepreneurs failed to mention concerned risks and risk minimization. Advisers appeared to be aware of the high failure rate among small businesses and the risks involved in developing a business. Each of the advisers recommended one tip which was intended to minimize a major risk and avert failure. Avoiding failure is obviously important but it was not always clear whether following risk minimization tips would actually contribute to business success.

The existence of risks seems to have been accepted as a simple fact of business life by the case studies. They were aware of the risks but accepted them and were used to them. As a result none of them found risk worthy of comment as a factor contributing to success. This is probably because many decisions in business life are risky. If risky decisions are unsuccessful they may lead to failure, but if they are successful they may not automatically make a major contribution to the development of the business. The entrepreneurs appear to believe that success is reliant on company actions rather than on passive methods of reducing risk. For this reason risk minimization has not been included as a key element contributing to success in the concluding section.

Two additional factors which the entrepreneurs in the case studies viewed as important are the workforce and hard work. These two practical features involved in running a small business were not mentioned by the advisers. There was unanimous agreement among all the case study companies that the quality and commitment of the workforce had a strong influence on success. Three of the four companies had adopted profit-sharing schemes as a method of rewarding loyalty and performance. Hard work, together with commitment, were thought to be beneficial throughout an organization, but their importance was greatest for the founder(s) and senior staff.

The final tip which received varying degrees of support was luck. It is perhaps surprising that all the preceding positive and constructive factors which contribute to enhancing company performance and minimizing external factors which might detract from success or contribute to failure should be influenced by an imponderable such as luck. Some of the contributors believe that luck can play a part in success. Other commentators argue that if a well-developed business strategy can be established using planning, marketing, hard work and a loyal workforce a company should develop a natural capacity to find and exploit business opportunities and make its own luck.

Conclusion

The preceding section compared the tips and advice given by all the advisers and case study entrepreneurs and identified five key elements of benefit to the successful development of a small business. In this concluding section it is therefore appropriate to combine these overall views and derive five tips for success. The importance of planning and marketing has been noted by all the contributors. Practical aspects of developing a successful small business were identified by all the case studies; tips concerning the workforce and hard work have therefore also been included. Limited controversy regarding the fifth tip – luck – was considered above. A sixth, risk minimization, has been noted as valuable advice but it has been excluded because it does not always appear to contribute actively to small business success. The five key tips which are an amalgamation of the tips and advice given by all the contributors are shown in Table 12.3.

The five tips should not be considered in isolation. Supporting recommendations, advice and strategies have been advocated by all the contributors. Their experiences and suggestions form a comprehensive source of information which should aid the successful development of any small business, whatever its criteria for success.

Criteria for small business success can vary between companies. This disparity in goals has been acknowledged throughout. The case studies, which have adopted a range of criteria for success, and the advisers who assist businesses with a wide range of views on success, have derived a common set of tips and

Table 12.3 Five tips for business success

(1) Adopt a clear business plan; carefully monitor the company's performance and changes in the market.
(2) Operate in a market which you know and understand.
(3) Maintain staff loyalty; policies and mechanisms for motivating staff are vital.
(4) Hard work and commitment from all staff are important.
(5) Be lucky; well-calculated planning and marketing can minimize risks and enhance luck.

strategies which should enhance success. None of the contributors specified particular tips or activities to achieve particular goals. It appears that this common set of tips and strategies is valuable for any company, whatever its motives for success. These tips and advice all contribute to developing what are generally regarded as well-run companies with sound operating practices and a loyal and committed workforce.

Index

financial
 analysts 51
 assistance 83
 consultancy 52
 control 42
 controls 40
 development 38
 goals 28
 growth 1, 5
 guarantee 45
 institutions 16, 48
 reward 4, 7, 27
 security 39, 106
 success 2, 19, 21, 29, 31, 98
 viewpoint 2, 30, 37
financiers 38
flashing beacons 28
Foley, Paul 27–35, 104
Fothergill S. 14, 18
founder 14
funding gap 38

GEC 34
geographical perspective 11
goals 4, 8, 27, 30, 58, 59, 97, 105, 108
Greater London 16
Growth Data Services Ltd 21, 22
Gudgin G. 14, 18, 26

Halfords 65
happiness 4, 27, 30
hardwork 100, 103, 108
high technology 3, 6, 47, 72, 86
 companies 2
 viewpoint 47
Hill Samuel Anniversary Award 20
hobbies 28, 32
Huddersfield 28

IBM UK Ltd 55
idiosyncratic business development 2
income 1, 5
independence 2–7, 28, 30, 52, 60, 79, 97, 98
Industrial and Commercial Finance Corporation 38
Industrial Common Ownership Fund 8
Industrial Common Ownership Movement 88
industrial heritage 16
Inland Revenue 57
Inner London Education Authority 56
innovation 2, 23, 62

 lack of 18
innovative firms 19
innovators 6
intercommunication systems 32
intuition 84
inventors 1, 6, 7, 62
investment 52
Investors in Industry PLC 55
invoices 66

Japanese imports 42
job
 creation 56
 dissatisfaction 81
 satisfaction 1–8, 27, 29, 87, 94, 97, 98
John Laing PLC 55

Keeble D. 13
Kent 21
Knaresborough 28
Kwik-Fit 2, 5, 64, 71, 97
Kwik-News 68

labour market 12
Lake District 6
Landis and Ghyr 81
large enterprises 14
leadership 40
Legal and General Group PLC 56
leisure 25
Lex Service PLC 56
licensing 41
Lloyd P. 18, 26
Lloyds bank 47
Lloyds Bowmaker Industrial Achievement Award 20
loan capital 39
Loan Guarantee Scheme 39, 57, 62
local authorities 39
Local Enterprise Agencies 39
local enterprise trusts 39
Local Investment Networking Company 57
location quotient 19
Loch Eil Outward Bound Centre 68
London 6, 32, 70
London Enterprise Agency 55
losses 58
Lovell, Peter 2, 55–63, 104
low technology 86
luck 79, 87, 95, 103

management 7, 35, 40, 67, 72